Soups & Stews

In the Kitchen with Bob

Soups &

Stews

Bob Bowersox

Food photographs by Mark Thomas Studio

QVC PUBLISHING, INC.

QVC Publishing, Inc.
Jill Cohen, Vice President and Publisher
Ellen Bruzelius, General Manager
Sarah Butterworth, Editorial Director
Karen Murgolo, Director of Acquisitions and Rights
Cassandra Reynolds, Publishing Assistant

Produced in association with Patrick Filley Associates, Inc.
Design by Joel Avirom and Jason Snyder
Photography by Mark Thomas Studio
Prop styling by Nancy Micklin
Food Styling by Ann Disrude

Q Publishing and colophon are trademarks of QVC Publishing, Inc.

Published by QVC Publishing, Inc., 50 Main Street, Mt. Kisco, New York 10549

Manufactured in Hong Kong

ISBN: 1-928998-04-6

First Edition

10 9 8 7 6 5 4 3 2 1

Contents

Introduction

Steaming bowls of soup are one of our favorite comfort foods. Satisfying and hearty, nutritious and restorative, light and refreshing, seasonal and savory, soups in all their glorious variety are essential to a good cook's repertoire everywhere in the world. You need only walk into a home filled with the aroma of a mouthwatering soup simmering on the stovetop to feel at ease and sense your taste buds being tantalized.

Soups are one thing I remember vividly about my childhood—rich chicken broth to nurse a cold, my mother's outstanding minestrone after a wintry afternoon in the backyard building a snowman, or chilled potato soup on a steamy July evening. Each one connects to a fond memory and inspires me to get out the stockpot to make soup for my own family. Nothing is more basic and satisfying to the senses—and the soul—than flavorful homemade soup.

Stews follow close on the heels of soup as a food that seems inherently consoling in cold weather, and immensely satisfying in any season. While soup can be defined in the most general terms as "a liquid savory dish, including broth, bisque and potage," and is made comparatively quickly, stews are marked by the "slow, steady cooking of a mixture of ingredients in a thick and opaque sauce."

Soups overlap with stews on occasion and vice versa, but both are a fundamental category of cooking everywhere in the world—and probably have been ever since the first cooking fire was lit. No wonder every language includes a word for "soup."

Soups and stews would seem to be a perfect food for our hectic world, designed to adapt to busy lives. Some soups can be made in minutes, and stews have the wonderful advantage of being assembled and then left to simmer away on their own while the cook goes on to another project.

Compiling the recipes for this cookbook, I was struck by the exhilarating variety of soups and stews Americans have adopted from different cultures—Thailand and other parts of Southeast Asia, India, China, Russia and Eastern Europe. Of course, we will always love our native gumbos, minestrones and chowders, and have taken to jambalaya with a passion, but no longer is soup made solely with vegetables and meat or poultry and served hot. We have cold soups and fruit soups. There are warm weather soups, cold weather soups, main dish soups, even dessert soups, soups that are served puréed and soups that are creamed. The variety is remarkable and the choices are exciting.

As an example, there's spicy Lemon Chicken Soup with its exotic blend of lemon, chilies and chicken, a collaboration of ingredients inspired by Thai kitchens. Even if you've never eaten at a Thai restaurant, it's appealing to all the senses. So is the Tomato Bread Soup, infused with herbs the way cooks in Tuscany have made it forever, and Zuppe di Pesce, another Italian classic, made with fresh white fish.

Stews also span the globe and reflect our changing tastes and familiarity with different flavors and ingredients, not to mention an American enthusiasm for spicier foods. Let's admit it. Stews like India's Lamb Korma with its pungent curry flavor, Morocco's classic Couscous Tajine with an exotic mix of savory and sweet ingredients seasoned by aromatic spices, and sizzling Chicken Creole, are downright exciting to eat. While they may take a bit longer to prepare, when you do take the time I guarantee that the thrilling tastes will be well worth the effort.

Anyone on a meatless or vegetarian diet will find a world of soups and stews in this collection. Many Asian, Indian and Middle Eastern soups and stews rely on lentils, barley, beans or chickpeas as their main protein source. From India comes Chickpea Stew, a tasty mélange of eggplant, tomatoes and chickpeas, plus delicious Spinach, Potato and Lentil Stew, a balanced, nutritious combination that wins honors as a main meal. Closer to home there's Spicy Red Bean Stew with its "red beans and rice" heritage from Louisiana's Cajun cuisine. I've included traditional vegetarian soups such as Garden Vegetable Soup and Vegetable Basil Soup, as well as some unusual ones like Finnish Summer Soup, a light soup packed with vegetables in a milk broth.

Fish soups and stews also cross geographic boundaries, so there is a wonderful assortment of this type included here, too. You'll find my grandmother's recipe for Zuppe di Pesce, a fish soup every coastal town in Italy adapted as its own, San Francisco's irresistible Cioppino, a classic Bouillabaisse from France, and a thoroughly American-style Crab and Rice Chowder, among others. In the fish stew category, there's Grouper Creole with spicy Caribbean flavors from lime and cumin, the Cajun Shrimp Etouffée, plus New England-inspired Fisher's Island Stew and 'Sconset Stew. I recommend them all!

Whichever soup or stew you choose to begin your adventure in this most satisfying of culinary categories, always select the freshest ingredients. Soups, particularly, are not intended to be made from leftovers, unless using bones for stock. I always advise using seasonal ingredients, since they create a soup or stew's essential character, reflecting the climate and the world around us as they tantalize our senses.

I hope you and your family enjoy this collection of soups and stews throughout the year. These recipes will inspire memorable meals whether winter winds are blustery, leaves are swirling to the ground, or it's a balmy summer evening by the shore.

SOUPS

Scotch Broth	Egg Drop Soup
Cheddar and Ale Soup with Sausage	Finnish Summer Soup
Ham and Red Lentil Soup	Vegetable Basil Soup
Hungarian Meatball Soup	Butternut Squash Soup
Mushroom and Barley Soup	Tomato Rosemary Soup
Quick Consommé	Potato Leek Soup
Lemon Chicken Soup	Gingered Pear Soup
Chicken and Corn Chowder	Curried Cauliflower Soup
Harvest Turkey Soup	Albuquerque Corn Soup
Turkey Vegetable Soup	Green Onion and Shiitake Soup

Scotch Broth

SERVES 6 TO 8

FROM THE RUGGED AND WINDY HIGHLANDS of Scotland comes this classic soup designed to warm you all the way to your toes and fingertips. A centuries old recipe, it's traditionally made with lamb, which has long been a Scottish staple, nutty-flavored pearl barley, and humble garden vegetables like rutabaga, carrots and onion. Simmer the ingredients for a few hours and you'll have a hearty soup that makes a full meal all on its own.

2 pounds lamb shoulder, cut into large pieces

3 quarts water

1 onion, diced

2 carrots, diced

1 leek, thinly sliced

½ cup rutabaga, diced

½ cup barley

1 bay leaf

1 teaspoon dry thyme

½ teaspoon salt

Place the lamb and water in a large pot and bring to a boil over high heat. Skim off any gray foam which rises to the surface. Add the remaining ingredients and bring to a boil. Lower the heat to a simmer and cook the soup for 2 hours. Remove the meat from the bone, dice, and return to the soup.

Serve with buttermilk biscuits.

Cheddar and Ale Soup with Sausage

SERVES 6 TO 8

THIS STURDY SOUP IS a man-pleaser, and as such it's perfect for a crowd of football fans, whether served in front of the T.V. or at a tailgate party. The robust flavors of garlic, balsamic vinegar, ale and assorted seasonings balance the distinctive tastes of kielbasa sausage, tomatoes and cheese in a delicious creamy soup that will have everyone asking for seconds. Remember to slowly stir in the cheese so it's completely blended with the broth.

   3   tablespoons butter

   ¾   cup plus 2 tablespoons minced shallots

   2   garlic cloves, minced

   3   tablespoons flour

2½   cups chicken stock, heated

1½   cups ale

1½   cups shredded white cheddar cheese

   ½   cup heavy cream

   ½   teaspoon salt

   ½   teaspoon freshly ground pepper

   3   ounces cooked kielbasa,
        cut into ¼-inch dice

   1   tomato, peeled, chopped

   2   tablespoon olive oil

   1   tablespoon balsamic vinegar

   1   tablespoon minced fresh basil

Melt the butter in a large pot over medium heat. Add ¾ cup shallots and garlic. Sauté until tender, about 5 to 7 minutes. Stir in the flour and cook for 5 minutes. Gradually add the hot chicken stock and ale, whisking until well incorporated. Bring to a simmer and cook for 10 minutes. Stir in the cheese, a handful at a time, until melted and smooth. Add the remaining ingredients and cook until the soup begins to simmer.

Serve with garlic bread (see recipe on page 122).

Ham and Red Lentil Soup

SERVES 6 TO 8

LENTILS HAVE BEEN CULTIVATED SINCE ANTIQUITY in Egypt and other parts of the Near East. The edible seeds of a legume plant, lentils come in various sizes and colors. Red lentils, actually a beautiful bright salmon color, are the most common variety. Among vegetables, lentils have the second highest protein level, after soy beans, which is why they are so highly valued in Asia. Simmered slowly with garlic, onion, celery and diced ham, the lentils soften and add an earthy flavor to this soup.

2 cloves garlic, minced

1 onion, diced

2 tablespoons olive oil

1 bay leaf

2 celery stalks, thinly sliced

2 cups red lentils, rinsed

½ pound ham, diced

2 quarts chicken stock

½ teaspoon salt

1 teaspoon freshly ground pepper

In a large, heavy pot, over medium heat, sauté the garlic and onion in the olive oil until soft, about 5 minutes. Add the bay leaf and celery and cook for another 3 to 5 minutes. Add the remaining ingredients and raise the heat to high. Bring to a boil, then lower the heat until the soup simmers. Cook for 1½ hours.

Serve with garlic bread (see recipe on page 122).

Hungarian Meatball Soup

SERVES 6

FROM PASTRIES TO PASTA, Hungary has a lavish culinary history of which its soups are just a small piece. In the 16th and 17th centuries, conquering Turks introduced foods like paprika, phyllo dough for strudels, and pilafs. Meatballs joined the menu during the Austro-Hungarian era when German cooking was influential.

Starring here, savory meatballs combine with potatoes and mushrooms in a satisfying main dish soup.

1	pound ground chuck
2	teaspoons tomato paste
1	teaspoon dry mustard
1	cup dry breadcrumbs
1	egg, beaten
½	teaspoon salt
2	tablespoons butter
1	onion, halved, thinly sliced
½	pound mushrooms, sliced
1	teaspoon paprika
4	cups beef stock
1	cup peeled, diced potatoes
	Sour cream for garnish

In a medium-size bowl, combine the chuck, tomato paste, mustard, breadcrumbs, egg and salt, and shape into 1-inch balls. In a large, heavy pot, over medium heat, melt the butter. Add the onion and mushrooms and sauté for / to 10 minutes. Add the paprika and stock, raise the heat and bring to a boil. Lower the heat and add the meatballs and potatoes and simmer gently for 30 minutes. Serve with a dollop of sour cream in each bowl.

Accompany with buttermilk biscuits (see recipe on page 124).

Mushroom and Barley Soup

SERVES 6 TO 8

BARLEY IS ONE OF THOSE ANCIENT cereal grains of the Near East that's now used primarily for brewing beer. When barley is called for in cooking, it's generally "pearl barley." This is barley that has been hulled and milled until it resembles small, glistening pearls. Barley used in soups is a tradition of the British Isles, one that's reprised here with a variety of vegetables and mushrooms in a hearty stock made from beef chuck and veal knuckle.

2 tablespoons corn oil

2 carrots, sliced

1 stalk celery, sliced

1 onion, chopped

2 cloves garlic, minced

2 parsnips, peeled, sliced

1 bay leaf

1 teaspoon dried thyme

1 pound mushrooms, quartered

2 pounds beef chuck, cut into 1- to 1½-inch cubes

1 veal knuckle (about 1 pound), cut into 1-inch cubes

2 quarts beef broth

½ cup barley

1 cup hot water

1 teaspoon salt

Heat the corn oil in a large, heavy pot over medium heat. Add the carrots, celery, onion, garlic and parsnips and sauté for 7 to 10 minutes, until the vegetables are soft. Add the bay leaf, thyme and mushrooms and cook for another 3 to 5 minutes. Add the beef and cook until it is slightly brown on all sides, about 7 to 10 minutes. Add the veal knuckle and beef broth, raise the heat to high until the soup boils. Lower the heat to a simmer and cook for 1 hour.

While the soup is cooking, soak the barley in the hot water and salt. Add the barley and simmer the soup for another half hour.

Serve with whole wheat quick bread (see recipe on page 123).

Quick Consommé

THIS CLEAR, SIMPLE SOUP, a favorite term in French cookbooks since the 16th century, refers to a "finished" soup, or one that has been "completed," unlike a stock or broth which is treated as an ingredient. Served hot or cold, consommé most often begins a meal to set the stage for more elaborate dishes. My streamlined version here has the sophisticated flavor of a classic clarified consommé, but doesn't require the traditional lengthy simmering time.

6 cups beef broth

3 egg whites

6 ounces ground sirloin of beef

4 peppercorns

½ teaspoon salt

¼ cup sherry

5 green onions, finely sliced

Place the broth in a large pot. Bring to a boil. In a medium bowl, mix together the egg whites, beef, peppercorns and salt.
Place this "raft" (meat mixture) in the broth and stir well. Let the raft rise to the surface and lower the heat to a gentle simmer. Cook for 1 hour and then strain through cheesecloth. Add the sherry and sprinkle with the green onions before serving.

Serve with thin slices of French bread.

Lemon Chicken Soup

SERVES 6 TO 8

WHILE SOME SOUPS ARE DEPENDENT upon the seasons for their ingredients, this one uses items available year-around in the produce department. Lemons, fresh ginger, hot chili peppers and tomatoes marry their flavors with chicken in a zesty soup that's influenced by the kitchens of Thailand. It's light and a bit exotic, with fusion flavors from all over Asia. Garnished with a bit of cilantro, it will delight the senses.

4 cups chicken stock

1 1-inch peel of lemon zest, pith removed

1 1-inch piece gingerroot, thinly sliced

6 tablespoons lime juice

1½ teaspoons chili paste

¾ pound tomatoes, cut into 1-inch chunks

1 pound skinless boneless chicken breast, cut into ¼-inch wide strips

2 jalapeño peppers, julienned

Fresh cilantro leaves for garnish

In a large pot, bring the chicken stock to a boil. Add the lemon zest, ginger and 2 tablespoons lime juice. Boil for 1 minute, add the chili paste and reduce the heat to medium. Add the tomatoes, cook for 1 minute and add the chicken strips. Stir occasionally. Simmer for 5 minutes, until the chicken is cooked but not overdone. Add the remaining 4 tablespoons of lime juice, jalapeño pepper, stir and remove from the heat. Garnish with the cilantro leaves before serving.

Serve with triangles of pita bread.

Chicken and Corn Chowder

SERVES 6 TO 8

CHOWDERS DERIVE THEIR NAME FROM the French word chaudiére, *meaning a large iron cooking pot used by fishermen in Breton, France, as well as by 18th century settlers in the Maritime Provinces of Canada. No doubt the word and the soup traveled south to New England's shores where chowders have long reigned supreme. In both areas, chowder always refers to a hearty soup. While traditionally made with seafood, there are delicious exceptions, as this chicken and corn variation testifies.*

3 cups fresh or frozen corn kernels

3 ounces bacon, diced

3 tablespoons butter

1 pound skinless boneless chicken breast, cut into ½-inch cubes

¾ cup finely chopped onions

½ cup finely chopped celery

2 cups ½-inch dice potatoes

4 cups chicken stock

1 cup heavy cream

1 tablespoon finely chopped fresh parsley for garnish

In a food processor or blender, puree 2 cups of the corn.

In a medium skillet, over medium heat, brown the bacon. When crisp, remove to a paper towel and discard the fat.

Melt the butter in a large pot over medium-high heat. Add the chicken and brown on all sides, about 5 to 7 minutes. Add the onions and celery and cook for another 5 minutes, until the vegetables are soft. Add the puréed corn kernels, potatoes and chicken stock. Raise the heat to high and bring to a boil. Reduce the heat until the soup simmers. Cover partially. Simmer for 20 minutes, until the potatoes are tender and the chicken is cooked through. Stir in the cream and simmer for another 3 minutes. Garnish with the parsley and bacon.

Serve with buttermilk biscuits (see recipe on page 124).

Harvest Turkey Soup

SERVES 6

TURKEY IS A WONDERFUL BASE TO CREATE a soup with anytime of the year, but especially after the holidays when using up leftovers and one more turkey sandwich is too much. Step out of the norm and make this hearty turkey vegetable soup with genuine southwestern flair. Instead of traditional vegetables like carrots or cauliflower, use corn, chilies and cilantro to give onions, tomatoes and potatoes a zesty new twist. Don't expect this satisfying soup to last for long, it will get gobbled up in no time!

2   pounds skinless boneless turkey breast, cut into bite-size pieces

6   cups turkey or chicken broth

1   medium onion, finely chopped

2   medium tomatoes, diced

½   teaspoon dried oregano

1   teaspoon grated lemon peel

¼   teaspoon freshly ground pepper

2   medium red potatoes, cut into 1-inch dice

1   8-ounce can sweet corn kernels

⅓   cup chopped fresh cilantro

2   medium mild red or green chilies, seeded, finely chopped

1   small ripe avocado

2   tablespoons lime juice

6   lime wedges for garnish

In a large pot, place the turkey, broth, onion, tomatoes, oregano, lemon peel and pepper. Bring to a boil over medium-high heat. Reduce the heat until the soup simmers and cook for 10 minutes. Add the potatoes and simmer for another 10 minutes. Add the corn, cilantro and chilies.

Peel and remove the pit of the avocado. Cut into ½-inch dice and toss with the lime juice. Just before serving, sprinkle each bowl with some of the avocado. Garnish with a wedge of lime.

Serve with a basket of tortilla chips.

Turkey Vegetable Soup

IN OUR HOUSEHOLD, MAKING A simmering pot of turkey soup after Thanksgiving was just as much a holiday ritual as glazing the turkey for its grand entrance at the family feast. In spite of the long list of ingredients, is well worth the effort of peeling and chopping. These days you can also buy turkey parts to cook the soup with and skip having to roast an entire bird.

1 tablespoon olive oil

2 cloves garlic, minced

35 ounces canned tomatoes with their juices, chopped

1½ pounds potatoes, peeled, cut into 1-inch dice

2 carrots, peeled, coarsely chopped

10 ounces pearl onions, peeled

2 stalks celery, finely chopped

¼ cup chopped mushrooms

1 teaspoon dried oregano

½ teaspoon dried rosemary

1 bay leaf

2 strips orange zest

½ teaspoon salt

1 turkey drumstick and 1 turkey thigh, skinned

10 ounces fresh or frozen green beans, cut into 1-inch pieces

1½ cups fresh or frozen corn kernels

3 cups chicken stock

⅓ cup chopped fresh parsley

In a large pot, warm the oil over medium heat. Add the garlic and sauté for 1 minute. Add all the remaining ingredients, except the parsley. Simmer gently for ½ hour, adding more chicken stock as needed to keep the soup liquid. Remove the turkey pieces and pull the meat off the bones. Set the meat aside and return the bones to the soup. Simmer for another ½ hour. Remove the bones from the soup, add the turkey meat and parsley and cook for 5 minutes more.

Serve with corn bread (on page 122).

Egg Drop Soup

SERVES 5

I have always loved this simple, elegant soup from China. I first tasted it when I was in my early twenties. Someone dared me to try it, and bet that I wouldn't. Not only did I win the bet, I also found a new love in this delicious, satisfying soup. I've tried a number of recipes—always seeking the "best one" yet. I think I've found it here.

1   egg

2   egg whites

6   cups chicken broth

1   tablespoon soy sauce

1   tablespoon oyster sauce

1   tablespoon sherry

½   tablespoon kosher salt

3   tablespoons cornstarch mixed with ¼ cup water

Put the egg and egg whites into a small bowl and set aside. Bring the broth to a boil, then reduce to a simmer and add the soy sauce, oyster sauce, sherry, and salt. Slowly add the cornstarch mixture until the soup thickens and clears.

Lightly beat the eggs until broken up but not bubbly. Remove the soup from the heat and immediately pour the eggs in a low and steady circular stream, while stirring the soup constantly. Serve immediately.

Accompany with pita bread wedges.

Finnish Summer Soup

SERVES 6

LIVING IN THE FAR NORTH, long, dark winters make the Finns crave their endless summer nights when gardens brim with fresh vegetables. In Finland, even the first new potato is cause for revelry. This traditional soup celebrates summer's bountiful harvest with a medley of vegetables simmered in a light, creamy broth until just crisp-tender. This soup is so good, it's also worth making in colder months using frozen vegetables to substitute for any that aren't available fresh.

2 cups water

1 teaspoon salt

4 small red potatoes, quartered

Pinch white pepper

1 tablespoon butter

3 small onions, coarsely chopped

6 small carrots, sliced

¼ pound green beans, cut into ½-inch pieces

1 cup fresh or frozen peas

1 cup half-and-half

1½ tablespoons flour

In a 5-quart pot, over high heat, bring the water and salt to a boil. Add the potatoes and simmer for 5 minutes. Add the white pepper, butter, onions, carrots, and green beans and simmer for 8 to 10 minutes more. Add the peas and simmer for 2 minutes. In a small bowl, stir together the half and half and the flour. Add to the soup and simmer for about 5 minutes, until the soup is slightly thickened.

Serve with a tomato salad.

VARIATION:
To serve as a chilled soup, allow it to come to room temperature, stirring occasionally, then cover and refrigerate for at least 2 hours.

Vegetable Basil Soup

IN MIDSUMMER, I THINK it's a luxury to bring home a basket of fresh produce from the farmers' market. Inspired by the seasonal bounty, I created this savory soup that takes maximum advantage of the wonderful variety of locally grown, fresh vegetables. Feel free to substitute or add vegetables to showcase what's in your local market, or in your own garden. And when you crave a taste of summer in colder months, by all means, use frozen vegetables to make this soup.

2   tablespoons olive oil

1   onion, chopped

1   celery stalk, sliced

1   carrot, sliced

1   potato, peeled, cut into $\frac{1}{2}$-inch cubes

2   cups peeled, chopped tomatoes

6   cups chicken or vegetable stock

1   cup cauliflower florets

2   small zucchini, sliced

$\frac{1}{2}$ pound fresh or frozen peas

$\frac{1}{3}$ cup chopped fresh basil

$\frac{1}{2}$ teaspoon salt

$\frac{1}{2}$ teaspoon freshly ground pepper

1   cup grated Parmesan cheese
    for garnish

In a 6- to 8-quart pot, over medium heat, warm the olive oil. Add the onion, celery and carrot and sauté, stirring occasionally, until they are soft but not brown, about 10 minutes. Add the potato, tomatoes and stock, cover and simmer for 15 minutes. Add the cauliflower and zucchini and cook for 10 minutes. Stir in the peas, basil, salt and pepper and cook for another 5 minutes. Sprinkle with Parmesan cheese.

Serve with garlic bread (see recipe on page 122).

Butternut Squash Soup

SERVES 6 TO 8

I LOVE THIS SMOOTH, SATINY SOUP in Autumn when days grow colder and a whole assortment of beautiful squashes comes into the market. I've selected butternut squash here since it steams quickly, but you can experiment with other varieties, too. This soup with its pumpkin pie spices is so easy and fast to make, that it seems like it should be on the menu once a week—at least. If you like, double the amounts and freeze a batch to serve later.

½ cup ¼-inch dice butternut squash

4 cups 1-inch dice butternut squash

1 onion, diced

5 cups chicken or vegetable stock

½ cup honey

1 tablespoon dried savory

¼ teaspoon freshly grated nutmeg or ground

¼ teaspoon cinnamon

½ teaspoon salt

¼ teaspoon white pepper

2 tablespoons chopped fresh chives for garnish

In a small pot, bring an inch of water to a boil. Add the small diced squash and cook for 1 minute. Drain and pat dry on a paper towel. Set aside for garnish.

Place the large dice squash and onion in a steamer basket over boiling water. Cover and steam for 10 minutes. While the vegetables are steaming, bring the chicken stock to a boil. When the squash and onion are tender, puree in a blender or food processor. Add the honey, savory, nutmeg, cinnamon, salt and white pepper. Blend well. Scrape the mixture into the chicken stock and stir to combine. Simmer gently for 5 minutes. Garnish with the chives.

Serve with oat muffins (see recipe on page 125).

Tomato Rosemary Soup

SERVES 6

I LOVE TO MAKE THIS SOUP when the garden is overflowing with the summer's bonanza of tomatoes. The heady fresh tomato fragrance is unrivaled and the hint of rosemary so enticing. If you don't have tomato plants in your backyard, check your farmers' market or grocery store. You may even be able to find some heirloom tomato varieties to try. If not, use Roma or plum tomatoes since these are the most flavorful among the supermarket offerings.

2	tablespoons olive oil
1	large onion, chopped
2	cloves garlic, chopped
6	large tomatoes, seeded, diced
½	cup dry white wine
2½	cups chicken or vegetable stock
1	4-inch rosemary sprig
½	teaspoon freshly ground pepper
	Salt to taste
¼	cup chopped green onions

In a large pot, over medium-high heat, warm the oil. Add the onion and garlic and sauté, stirring occasionally, for 5 minutes. Add the tomatoes, white wine, stock, rosemary sprig and pepper. Raise the heat to high and bring to a boil. Lower the heat until the soup simmers and cook, uncovered, for 45 minutes. Turn off the heat and allow the soup to cool down until it's warm. Take out the rosemary sprig. Remove half of the soup and puree in a blender or food processor until smooth. Return the puree to the soup and stir until combined. Season with salt to taste and sprinkle with the green onions.

Accompany with garlic toasts.

VARIATION:
To serve as a chilled soup, allow it to come to room temperature, stirring occasionally, then cover and refrigerate for at least 2 hours.

Potato and Leek Soup

SERVES 6 TO 8

IN ITS MOST REFINED FORM, a chilled soup of puréed potatoes and leeks thickened with cream is called Vichyssoise , which despite its thoroughly French name was created in New York City around 1917 by a French chef. Sprinkled with chopped fresh chives, it was considered the ultimate in sophisticated luncheon soups. My version here features the same complimentary pairing of leeks and potatoes, but in a more casual preparation. Whether you serve it hot or cold, this smooth, velvety soup is always satisfying.

1 large potato, peeled, diced

1 cup chopped leeks, white part only

3 cups chicken or vegetable stock

½ teaspoon salt

1 cup half-and-half

½ teaspoon white pepper

1 teaspoon sweet paprika

Corn oil

1 onion, cut into thin rings, separated

In a large pot, over high heat, bring the potato, leeks, stock and salt to a boil. Lower the heat to a simmer and cook for 15 to 20 minutes, until the potatoes are tender. Remove from the heat. Using a blender or food processor, puree the soup with the half-and-half in batches. Return to the pot and bring to a simmer over medium heat. Whisk in the white pepper and paprika.

In a shallow skillet, over high heat, heat the corn oil until a drop of water will spatter when dropped into it. Add the onion rings and fry until golden brown. Remove to paper towels with a slotted spoon.

Garnish each bowl with the fried onion rings.

Serve with oat muffins (see recipe on page 125).

VARIATION:

To serve as a chilled soup, allow it to come to room temperature, stirring occasionally, then cover and refrigerate for at least 2 hours.

Gingered Pear Soup

FRUIT SOUPS ARE COMMON in Scandinavia where an abundance of summer berries has inspired a culinary tradition. Refreshing and light, fruit soups are surprisingly versatile and can be served either cold or hot depending on the season. In either form, they're a delightful way to begin a meal, to cleanse the palate between courses, or star as a distinctive dessert. Choose perfectly ripe Anjou, Bartlett or Comice pears with their intense flavor to balance the fresh ginger in this chilled soup.

6	firm pears, peeled, halved, stem and seeds removed
4	cups white wine
¼	cup honey
1	vanilla bean
1	cinnamon stick
4	whole cloves
1	2½-inch slice gingerroot, peeled
¼	cup shredded Monterey Jack cheese for garnish

In a large pot, over high heat, poach the pears in the wine with the honey, vanilla bean, cinnamon stick, cloves and ginger for about 40 to 45 minutes, until the pears are soft. Drain over a large bowl to save the poaching liquid. Puree the pears in a blender or food processor and discard the other solid ingredients. With the blender or food processor running, add 3 cups of the poaching liquid. Serve with a sprinkling of the cheese in each bowl.

Serve with Monterey Jack cheese toasts.

VARIATION:
To serve as a chilled soup, allow it to come to room temperature, stirring occasionally, then cover and refrigerate for at least 2 hours.

Curried Cauliflower Soup

SERVES 6

AROMATIC CURRY ENHANCES the delicate flavors of cauliflower and leeks in this sophisticated vegetable soup. With a nod towards Indian cuisine where sautéed, curried cauliflower is a favorite dish, this soup is a novel way for Westerners to experience this vegetable. Look for an Indian curry powder to enjoy the richest curry flavor, and be sure to let the soup rest for five minutes before serving so that its flavors can fully blend.

4	tablespoons olive oil
3	medium leeks, trimmed, thinly sliced, carefully washed
5	cloves garlic
4	tablespoons curry powder
7	cups water
2	medium cauliflower heads, broken into florets
⅓	cup Madiera wine
1	teaspoon salt
1	cup half-and-half
½	cup minced fresh parsley

In a heavy skillet, heat the oil over medium heat. Add the leeks, garlic and curry powder and sauté for 5 to 7 minutes.

In a large pot, bring the water, cauliflower, Madiera and salt to a boil. Stir in the leek mixture and simmer the soup for 20 minutes. Stir in the half-and-half and parsley. Return to a gentle simmer, remove from the heat and let stand 5 minutes before serving.

Serve with papadums roasted until lightly browned about 3 inches above an open flame.

Albuquerque Corn Soup

SERVES 6

FLAVORS AND INGREDIENTS of the Southwest mingle in this zesty soup that can be made using canned corn, or by shaving kernels off corn on the cob. Either preparation is equally delicious. Add more or less chili peppers to temper the soup's "heat" to your personal taste. Served with a green salad and hot buttermilk biscuits, this soup is always one of my family's favorites for Sunday night supper.

¼ cup butter

4 cups fresh or frozen corn kernels

1 clove garlic, minced

1 cup chicken or vegetable broth

2 cups milk

1 teaspoon dried oregano

4 ounces canned diced green chili peppers

1 teaspoon salt

1 cup shredded Monterey Jack cheese

Fresh cilantro for garnish

Melt the butter over medium heat in a 5- to 6-quart pot. Add the corn and garlic and cook, stirring often, until the corn is browned, about 7 to 10 minutes. Remove from the heat. Place half of the corn and the broth in a blender. Puree until smooth. Return the corn mixture to the pot, and stir in the milk, oregano and chilies. Bring to a boil and remove from the heat. Stir in the salt and cheese. Garnish with the cilantro.

Serve with corn bread (see recipe on page 122).

Green Onion and Shiitake Soup

SERVES 6 TO 8

CREAM OF MUSHROOM SOUP was never so elegant and delicious as when made with flavorful shiitake mushrooms. Both fresh and dried versions of this golden brown mushroom are used here, so their earthy essence permeates the soup's rich base of cream and chicken stock. Sautéed green onions add a crisp counterpoint. You'll find the fresh form of these cultivated Japanese mushrooms in the produce section of most good markets, and dried ones in the Asian food section.

8	dried shiitake mushrooms
6	cups chicken or vegetable stock
4	bunches green onions, sliced, including tops
2	cloves garlic, crushed
¼	cup butter
3	tablespoons flour
1	cup heavy cream
¼	teaspoon salt
¼	teaspoon freshly ground pepper
3	to 4 fresh shiitake mushrooms, sliced for garnish

In a large bowl, soak the dried shiitake mushrooms in warm water until they are puffy and tender, about 30 minutes. Cut off any hard stems, press out excess water, and slice the tops into ¼-inch strips.

In a large pot, bring the chicken stock to a boil. Add the mushroom strips, lower the heat and simmer for 20 minutes. While the stock is simmering, sauté the green onions and garlic in the butter, over medium heat, in a large pot for about 10 minutes. Add the flour, stir until smooth and cook for 3 to 5 minutes. Remove from the heat. Add the chicken and mushroom stock to the scallion and garlic mixture, a cup at a time, stirring well before each addition until all of the stock is incorporated. Return to the heat and simmer for 12 to 15 minutes, until the soup is thick and smooth.

Temper the cream by adding about ½ cup of the hot soup and stirring well. Then add the cream into the hot soup and stir to blend. Season with salt and pepper and garnish with some slices of fresh shiitake.

Serve with French bread.

Georgian Soup with Fresh Herbs

SERVES 6

GEORGIA, BORDERED BY TURKEY, Armenia and Azerbaijan, is the northernmost country in the Caucasus region. Enjoying a Mediterranean-like climate, it shares culinary traditions with both Turkey and Persia. Georgian cuisine is considered a major influence on Russian cookery styles since the country was long part of the Russian Empire and the Soviet Union. This simple, creamy soup, thickened with beaten eggs in the traditional Georgian manner, is subtly flavored with fresh herbs added just before serving.

2 tablespoons butter

½ cup chopped shallots

6 cups chicken or vegetable stock

2 tablespoons flour

2 large eggs

¼ teaspoon sugar

1 tablespoon white wine vinegar

2 tablespoons chopped fresh tarragon

3 tablespoons chopped fresh cilantro

½ teaspoon salt or to taste

Croutons for garnish (optional)

In a large, heavy pot, over medium heat, melt the butter. Add the shallots and sauté for 4 to 5 minutes, until they are soft. Raise the heat and add 4½ cups of the stock and bring to a boil. In a small bowl, whisk together the flour with 1 cup of the remaining stock and gradually add to the boiling soup. Reduce the heat and simmer for 10 minutes. Remove from the heat and allow to cool.

In a medium bowl, whisk together the eggs with the remaining ½ cup of stock. Add the sugar and vinegar and beat well. Gradually pour about 1 cup of the warm soup into the egg mixture, whisking constantly. Slowly add the egg mixture back into the soup, whisking constantly, and heat until just below the simmering point for 45 seconds. Remove from the heat and add the fresh herbs and salt. Garnish with croutons, if desired.

Serve with cheese toasts (see recipe on page 123).

Chinese Vegetable Noodle Soup

SERVES 6

A FULL-BODIED HOMEMADE chicken stock is a must for this light, Asian-inspired, clear soup packed with crisp vegetables. Traditional ingredients like sesame oil, soy sauce and ginger give the broth its distinctive flavor. Once you have the vegetables prepared, this soup is a snap to make and ready to serve in about ten minutes. If you live near an Asian market, look for thin rice noodles to substitute for the pasta noodles.

5	cups chicken stock
¼	cup dry white wine
1	tablespoon sesame oil
1	teaspoon ground ginger
1	tablespoon soy sauce
1	carrot, peeled, thinly sliced on the bias
6	snow peas, sliced width-wise
¼	cup small cauliflower pieces
¼	cup chopped broccoli
½	cup sliced mushrooms
½	cup fresh or frozen peas
6	ounces fettuccini noodles, broken into 3-inch pieces

In a large pot, over high heat, bring the stock, wine, sesame oil, ginger and soy sauce to a boil. Add the vegetables and noodles and simmer for about 10 minutes, until the noodles are tender. Serve in bowls.

Serve with toasted pita wedges dusted with Parmesan cheese.

Pasta e Fagioli

SERVES 4

My wife Toni, being half Italian, "knows from Pasta e Fagioli." You can't pass a non-authentic Fagioli by her. While there are a dozen great canned soups out there, the best way to taste a Pasta e Fagioli the way it was meant to be tasted, is to make it yourself. Here's a recipe that's passed muster at our house.

1½ teaspoons olive oil

1 cup chopped onions

2 cloves garlic, minced

1 rib celery, chopped

1 carrot, chopped

2 cups drained, rinsed cooked white beans (cannellini)

1 14-ounce can whole tomatoes, drained, seeded, chopped

2 tablespoons chopped fresh parsley

4 cups chicken broth

½ teaspoon dried rosemary

½ teaspoon dried sage

½ teaspoon salt or to taste

¼ teaspoon freshly ground pepper or to taste

⅓ cup uncooked, small shaped pasta

Grated Parmesan cheese for garnish

Heat the oil in a large, heavy pot. Add the onion, garlic, celery and carrot. Cook over medium heat until the carrot softens, about 10 minutes. Keep the pot covered, stirring occasionally.

Slightly crush the beans in your hand as you drop them into the pot—you can do this by the handful, not bean by bean (you don't want all the beans crushed). Stir in the remaining ingredients except for the pasta and Parmesan cheese. Bring to a simmer and cook covered for 10 more minutes.

Stir in the pasta and continue to simmer until the pasta is cooked through, about 10 minutes more. Sprinkle with Parmesan cheese.

Serve with focaccia (see recipe on page 124).

Schee

SERVES 6

SIMPLE AND HEARTY ON ITS OWN, by the end of the 19th century Russian cooking included many elements of Slavic cuisine with its reliance on cabbage, sour cream, pork, potatoes and kasha, as well as culinary influences from France, Scandinavia, Turkey, and Germany. A steaming bowl of this basic, nourishing, old-style cabbage soup and a chunk of sour, dark bread would have been a typical peasant meal in Russia during Czarist days. A family's income determined whether or not it could afford a bone to add to the soup pot and for many it was only vegetables. Even today, Russians are fond of the saying, "Schee and kasha, that's our mother."

1	medium onion, thinly sliced
2	tablespoons butter
21	ounces beef broth
2½	cups coarsely shredded cabbage
2	medium carrots, sliced
1	medium potato, cut into ½-inch dice
½	stalk of celery, sliced
1	medium tomato, coarsely chopped
1	teaspoon salt
	Sour cream and fresh dill for garnish

In a large, heavy pot over medium heat, cook the onions in the butter until tender, about 10 minutes. Add the beef broth, cabbage, carrots, potatoes and celery. Bring to a boil. Cover and simmer until the vegetables are tender, about 20 minutes. Stir in the tomato and salt and simmer, uncovered for about 10 minutes.

Top each serving with a dollop of sour cream and a sprinkle of fresh dill.

Serve with whole wheat quick bread (see recipe on page 123).

Minestrone

SERVES 6

FEW SOUPS SPEAK OF ITALY more strongly than this classic vegetable and pasta soup that's easily a meal all by itself. Although thought to have originated in the Genoa area—where it is made with pumpkin, cabbage and Fava beans and garnished with three types of pasta—every region of Italy has its own version with slightly different ingredients. I watched my grandmother make this wonderful soup for years, and finally persuaded her to write down her method. Here it is.

1 tablespoon olive oil

1 cup chopped onion

¼ cup chopped celery

3 slices bacon, chopped

1 clove garlic, minced

½ teaspoon dried basil

½ teaspoon dried oregano

3 cups water

1 14-ounce can stewed tomatoes with their juices, chopped

½ cup drained, rinsed canned chickpeas

½ cup finely shredded white cabbage

½ cup coarsely chopped carrots

2 tablespoons minced fresh parsley

¼ cup broken spaghetti

In a large, heavy pot over medium heat warm the oil. Add the onion, celery, bacon, garlic, basil and oregano and sauté for 10 to 15 minutes or until tender and slightly browned. Add the water, tomatoes with their juices, chick peas, cabbage, carrots and parsley. Bring to a boil over high heat and the lower the heat until the soup simmers. Cover and cook for 20 to 30 minutes, until the cabbage and carrots are tender. Add the spaghetti. Return to a simmer and cook for another 10 minutes, until the spaghetti is tender.

Serve with Italian bread.

Cuban Black Bean Soup

SERVESS 6 TO 8

ONE OF MY FAVORITE SOUP EXPERIENCES came at the end of a cruise in the Caribbean, when Toni and I had a half day to kill in San Juan, Puerto Rico before our flight home. We decided to have lunch poolside at the Hotel San Juan (a fabulous place!), and we each ordered Cuban Black Bean Soup. We were in love with the soup from that moment on. It took a number of tries, combining several different recipes, but we finally re-created the taste and consistency of the soup we had that day in San Juan. It's a hearty, earthy soup, and one of my favorites.

1 pound dried black beans, cleaned, soaked overnight

6 cups water

4 cups chicken or vegetable stock

2 tablespoons olive oil

2 medium onions, finely diced

2 to 3 garlic cloves, minced

2 tablespoons vinegar

½ teaspoon ground cumin

1 teaspoon sugar

Salt and freshly ground black pepper to taste

1 onion, finely diced, for garnish

Sour cream for garnish

In a strainer, drain the soaked beans and rinse them lightly under cold running water. Put the beans and fresh water in a large stock pot, cover the beans with at least 2 inches of water, then cover and bring to a boil. When they reach a boil, reduce the heat to low and simmer for at least 2 hours, until the beans are tender enough to mash with a fork.

Remove 1 cup of the beans and 1 cup of the liquid from the pot and place in a blender. Puree the beans and liquid, then return the puree to the pot. Add the stock and return the soup to a low simmer.

Meanwhile, in a large skillet, heat the olive oil over medium-high heat, add the onions and cook until browned. Add the cooked onion and the garlic to the soup, cover the pot, and simmer for another 2 hours. Add the vinegar, cumin and sugar and let the soup simmer another 15 minutes. Add the salt and pepper to taste.

Serve garnished with the diced onion and the sour cream.

Accompany with corn bread (see recipe on page 122).

Soups

Tomato Bread Soup

SERVES 4 TO 6

WITH ORIGINS IN TUSCANY, this unusual thick and tasty soup makes a delicious case for never throwing bread away, and few Italians ever do, knowing well that good bread has a life longer than the day you buy it. In a country where well-crafted bread is sacred and food is rarely wasted, a bowl of this flavorful tomato soup with its herbal accents and a splash of pungent red wine vinegar is a stunning example of simple culinary genius and resourcefulness. Use either white or wheat bread.

1 pound country-style bread

3 tablespoons extra virgin olive oil

2 cloves garlic, thinly sliced

7 cups chopped, very ripe plum or beefsteak tomatoes

1 teaspoon fresh, chopped sage or ½ teaspoon dried

1 teaspoon chopped, fresh basil

½ teaspoon salt

½ teaspoon freshly ground pepper

3 to 4 cups vegetable stock

2 teaspoons red wine vinegar

⅓ cup extra virgin olive oil for garnish

Trim the crusts off the bread and cut into 1-inch cubes. Place in a single layer on a tray and dry overnight.

In a large pot, warm the olive oil over medium heat and sauté the garlic until it is soft, about 1 minute. Add the bread and cook for 2 minutes. Stir in the tomatoes and cook for about 5 to 7 minutes, until they begin to soften. Add the sage, basil, salt and pepper. Gradually add enough stock to keep the mixture soupy. Mash the bread with the back of a spoon to help it blend with the tomatoes. Gently simmer the soup for 30 to 40 minutes, being sure that no chunks of bread remain. Remove from the heat and let the soup rest for 30 to 60 minutes. Return the soup to a low heat and stir in the red wine vinegar. Simmer for 1 minute. Drizzle olive oil over the top of each bowl.

Serve with garlic bread (see recipe on page 122).

Roasted Red Pepper Soup

SERVES 6

The dusky red color and natural sweetness of this delicate soup are derived from roasted red bell peppers. Since it's so simple to roast and peel the peppers, I like to prepare a batch or two in advance to have on hand when the urge strikes to make this thick, puréed soup. It's equally delicious served hot or cold. Just remember not to overcook the mixture if you reheat the soup. A sprinkling of cilantro over each bowl intensifies the red pepper flavor.

6 large red bell peppers, halved, seeded

2 tablespoons butter

1 cup chopped shallots

¼ teaspoon red pepper flakes

1 cup dried white breadcrumbs

3 cups chicken or vegetable stock

½ cup heavy cream

½ teaspoon salt

⅓ cup chopped fresh cilantro for garnish

Place the red peppers, cut side down, on a baking sheet and cook 4 inches under the broiler until the skin begins to blacken and blister, 5 to 7 minutes. Remove from the oven and when cool enough to handle, peel the skin off the peppers. Coarsely chop the peppers.

In a deep skillet, over medium heat, melt the butter. Add the shallots and red pepper flakes and sauté for 5 minutes. Add the breadcrumbs and red peppers, stir well and cook for 3 to 5 minutes. Add the chicken stock and bring to a boil. Remove from the heat and allow to cool. Working in batches, puree the soup in a blender or food processor. Whisk in the heavy cream and salt and place over medium heat to bring the soup to a gentle simmer. Just before serving, sprinkle each bowl with the cilantro.

Serve with a basket of nacho chips.

VARIATION:
To serve as a chilled soup, allow it to come to room temperature, stirring occasionally, then cover and refrigerate for at least 2 hours.

Sweet Pea Soup

SERVES 6

SOME PEA SOUPS ARE MADE with ham hocks or bacon, but in this version, it's simply peas in the spotlight. While peas plucked fresh from a summer garden or the farmers' market and shelled by hand are sublime in this pureed soup, I think it's equally delicious using frozen peas. Green beans, zucchini and basil intensify the soup's color and flavor, while rice adds texture. This soup is excellent served hot, but it's also very refreshing served cold on a humid summer day.

⅓ cup olive oil

1 large onion, chopped

3 garlic cloves, chopped

2 cups chopped zucchini

1½ cups fresh or frozen peas

¼ pound green beans, chopped

⅓ cup rice

3 cups chicken or vegetable stock

¼ cup chopped fresh basil

1 cup skim milk

⅓ cup low-fat sour cream

½ teaspoon white pepper
   Salt to taste

2 tablespoons low-fat sour cream

2 to 3 teaspoons chicken or vegetable stock

In a large pot, over medium heat, warm the olive oil. Add the onion and garlic and sauté, stirring occasionally, for 5 minutes. Add the zucchini, peas and beans. Cover and cook for 10 minutes. Add the rice, stock and basil and bring to a simmer. Return the cover and simmer gently for 18 minutes. Remove from the heat and when cool enough to handle, puree in batches in a blender or food processor. Gradually add the skim milk and sour cream. Add the white pepper and salt to taste. Adjust the thickness with more skim milk.

Whisk together the remaining sour cream and chicken stock . Drizzle over the soup in a decorative pattern. Serve hot or warm.

Accompany with egg rolls.

VARIATION:

To serve as a chilled soup, allow it to come to room temperature, stirring occasionally, then cover and refrigerate for at least 2 hours. The soup will be thicker if served cold.

Manhattan Clam Chowder

SERVES 6

In New England there is constant conversation about what makes a genuine chowder. But on one point everyone agrees. Only chowders from New York and Baltimore contain tomatoes—a cause for scorn by true New England chowder lovers. Sometime in the 1930's the tomato variety of clam chowder, with its assorted vegetables and chunks of tender clams, came to be called "Manhattan." The following version has a bit of a kick to it from the splash of hot sauce.

2 slices bacon, diced

1 large onion, diced

1 celery stalk, sliced

1 carrot, peeled, sliced

1 teaspoon dried thyme

4 cups peeled, chopped tomatoes

1 cup corn kernels

2 drops hot pepper sauce (such as Tabasco)

2 cups fish stock

1 teaspoon salt

½ teaspoon freshly ground pepper

2 cups peeled, diced potatoes

1 pint fresh or canned clams, drained (reserve liquid), chopped

Oyster crackers

In a large, heavy pot, over medium heat, cook the bacon until it begins to brown, about 5 to 7 minutes. Add the onion and sauté for another 5 minutes. Add the celery, carrot and thyme and sauté for 3 minutes. Raise the heat to high and add the tomatoes, corn kernels, hot sauce, fish stock, salt, pepper and potatoes and bring to a boil. Lower the heat until the soup simmers and cook for 20 to 30 minutes, until the potatoes are tender. Add the clams and as much of the reserved liquid as needed and heat through. Remove from the heat and serve immediately. Serve with oyster crackers.

Accompany with French bread.

Zuppe di Pesce

ITALY'S BOOT-SHAPED PENINSULA dipping into the Mediterranean blessed the country with a long seacoast and as a consequence, every little coastal town has its own recipe for fish soup, or "zuppe di pesce." This recipe is very close to the one handed down by my grandmother who grew up on the Adriatic coast. Any firm and flaky white fish can be used in the soup. Choose from delicately flavored fish like cod, red snapper, sole or orange roughy to best compliment the soup's other delicate flavors.

¼   cup extra virgin olive oil

1   onion, peeled, chopped

2   cups chopped celery

5   cloves garlic, minced

1   tablespoon chopped fresh rosemary

2   tablespoons chopped fresh Italian parsley

8   cups fish stock or water (or a combination of both)

2   cups dry white wine

1   pound white-fleshed fish fillets, cut into 1-inch pieces

½   teaspoon salt

¼   teaspoon cayenne pepper

Heat the olive oil in a large pot over medium heat. Sauté the onion, celery and garlic until soft, about 10 minutes. Add the rosemary, parsley, stock and wine, and bring to a boil. Lower the heat until the soup simmers and cook for 10 minutes. Remove from the heat and press through a fine sieve or food mill. Return the soup to the pot and add the fish. Bring the soup to a simmer and cook for 8 to 10 minutes. Stir in the salt and cayenne.

Serve with focaccia (see recipe on page 124).

Bouillabaisse

SERVES 6 TO 8

CONSIDERED A SIMPLE FISHERMAN'S soup along Mediterranean shores, this fish soup is familiar in many areas, but is most often associated with the Provençal region of France. The word is actually a contraction of two French verbs: bouiller, *meaning "to boil," and* abaisser *meaning "to reduce." Despite all its regional variations, a traditional bouillabaisse recipe always includes a tremendous assortment of fish and shellfish, plus onions, garlic, tomatoes and parsley, and sometimes saffron. After that, anything goes, as long as it's fresh and flavorful.*

6 shallots, minced

2 cloves garlic, minced

3 tablespoons olive oil

1 bay leaf

¼ teaspoon dried thyme

½ teaspoon freshly ground pepper

¼ teaspoon crushed saffron

⅛ teaspoon cayenne pepper

¼ teaspoon crushed fennel seeds

1 orange rind, pith removed

3 pounds fish bones (heads and spine)

1 quart water

1 quart white wine

1 14-ounce can crushed tomatoes with their juices

2 pounds flounder fillet, cut into 2-inch pieces

2 pounds halibut fillet, cut into 2-inch pieces

2 dozen mussels, well scrubbed

2 dozen little neck clams, well scrubbed

In a large, heavy pot, over medium heat, sauté the shallots and garlic in the olive oil for 5 minutes. Add the bay leaf, thyme, pepper, saffron, cayenne pepper and fennel seeds and cook for another 3 to 5 minutes. Add the orange rind, fish bones, water and wine and bring to a boil over high heat. Reduce the heat until the broth simmers and cook for ½ hour. Strain the broth through a sieve into another large pot. Add the tomatoes and fish. Bring to a simmer over medium heat and cook for 10 minutes. Add the mussels and clams and cook until all the shellfish are opened, about 10 to 15 minutes.

Serve with garlic bread (see recipe on page 122).

Spicy Shrimp Gumbo

SERVES 6

THE NAME "GUMBO" COMES FROM an African word for okra, a ridged, tapering pod eaten as a vegetable. The word is also the name for a thick soup that's a staple in Cajun cooking, the sultry, spicy hot cuisine of Louisiana bayou country. Gumbos traditionally contain a variety of vegetables, seafood and meats, and may be thickened with sliced okra, as in this recipe, or filé (a powder made from dried sassafras leaves). Use fresh or frozen shrimp in this version for a taste of Creole cooking.

1	tablespoon corn oil
1	tablespoon flour
2	slices bacon, chopped
1	14½-ounce can stewed tomatoes
8	ounce bottle clam juice
1	cup chicken stock
1½	cups sliced fresh okra
1	teaspoon thyme
12	ounces medium shrimp, peeled, deveined
½	teaspoon hot sauce (such as Jamaican Jerk Sauce)

In a large, heavy pot, over medium heat, combine the oil and flour until it forms a "roux" or paste. Add the bacon. Stir until the roux turns a dark brown. Add the tomatoes, clam juice, chicken stock, okra and thyme. Break up the tomatoes. Reduce the heat, cover and simmer until okra is tender, about 20 minutes. Uncover and add the shrimp, hot sauce and simmer until the shrimp is coral pink, about 5 minutes.

Serve over cooked rice in a bowl and accompany with hush puppies (see recipe on page 125).

Oyster Chowder

IN THE 19TH CENTURY, picnics in coastal New England were often called "chowder parties" and served as family get-togethers, fundraisers for charity or political causes, and social gatherings by professional groups. Held on the beach, close to the source of fresh shellfish like clams and oysters, a steaming cauldron of chowder easily served a crowd. With or without potatoes, oyster chowders were enjoyed both for their prized ingredient and elegant taste.

4	slices bacon, chopped
1	onion, diced
1	celery stalk, thinly sliced
1	carrot, diced
½	red bell pepper, seeded, diced
1½	cups heavy cream
1½	cups chicken stock
1	cup dry white wine
½	teaspoon salt
¼	teaspoon white pepper
30	to 36 shucked oysters with their liquor
1	tablespoon chopped fresh Italian parsley
2	teaspoons chopped fresh tarragon

In a heavy pot, over medium heat, cook the bacon until it is crisp, about 5 minutes. Remove with a slotted spoon to a paper towel to drain. Add the onion, celery, carrot and bell pepper. Stir well. Cover and cook for 12 minutes, until the vegetables are soft. Add the cream, stock, wine, salt and pepper. Simmer gently for 5 to 7 minutes. Add the oysters and their liquor. Return the bacon to the pot and cook for another 5 minutes. Stir in the parsley and tarragon.

Serve with whole wheat quick bread (see recipe on page 123).

Crab and Rice Chowder

SERVES 6

NEW ENGLAND FISHERMEN BROUGHT HOME a great assortment of fresh seafood from the Atlantic, inspiring the region's famous chowders. Since other basic chowder ingredients were already in the larder, stirring up a pot of the hearty soup when fresh fish or shellfish arrived in the kitchen was simple. In this contemporary chowder, the ingredients are also easy to have on hand. Canned crab stars as the seafood, while a medley of vegetables and rice adds texture and taste to the light broth.

1 tablespoon corn oil

1 onion, finely chopped

8 ounces mushrooms, thinly sliced

½ teaspoon dried thyme

2 cups broccoli florets

1 red bell pepper, seeded, finely chopped

2 cups chicken broth

2 cups low-fat milk

1 17-ounce can cream-style corn

6 ounces crabmeat

3 cups cooked white rice

Salt and freshly ground pepper to taste

Heat the oil in a large pot over medium heat. Add the onion, mushrooms and thyme. Sauté, stirring often, until the vegetables begin to brown, about 5 to 7 minutes. Add the broccoli and red pepper and cook for another 5 minutes. Stir in the broth, milk and corn. Cook for 3 to 5 minutes, but do not allow to boil. Stir in the crab and rice and heat through, about 3 to 5 minutes. Season with salt and pepper.

Serve with buttermilk biscuits (see recipe on page 124).

57

Cioppino

SERVES 6

PAIR SAN FRANCISCO'S ITALIAN HERITAGE with a natural abundance of fish and shellfish on the Pacific Coast and it's not surprising that an enterprising cook would create this delicious fish soup. It soon became a favorite in restaurants and homes in the City by the Bay. Feel free to vary the fish and shellfish according to what's in season, but always buy the freshest available. The spicy tomato broth is a bold compliment to the mild sweetness of the shrimp, crab and white fish that everyone will enjoy.

4 cloves garlic, minced

¼ cup olive oil

1 medium onion, finely chopped

1 green bell pepper, seeded, chopped

1 tablespoon red wine vinegar

1½ cups dry white wine

1 teaspoon dried oregano

1 28-ounce can crushed tomatoes with their juices

2 shots hot sauce (such as Tabasco)

1 tablespoon tomato paste

½ pound medium shrimp, shelled, deveined

1 pound white fish fillet (such as cod, scrod, haddock)

1 pound crabmeat

1 teaspoon salt

½ teaspoon freshly ground pepper

2 tablespoons minced fresh parsley

In a large, heavy pot, over medium heat, sauté the garlic in the oil until it begins to brown, about 3 to 5 minutes. Add the onion and green pepper and cook 5 minutes. Add the vinegar and boil. Add the wine and oregano and simmer for 5 minutes. Add the tomatoes, hot sauce and tomato paste and bring to a boil. Add the shrimp and white fish and simmer until the shrimp turns coral pink, about 5 minutes. Stir in the crabmeat and heat until just warmed through. Adjust the seasoning with salt and pepper. Sprinkle each serving with parsley.

Serve with a French bread.

Beef Stock

THREE TYPES OF STOCK (white stock from poultry, brown stocks from meats, and vegetable stock), are traditionally used to flavor sauces, stews or braised dishes and often as a base for soups. In this case, when preparing a meat stock, browning beef bones in the oven is an easy way to increase their flavor before adding liquid. For a lightly flavored stock, use only the bones. But if a richer stock is desired, choose bones that still have meat attached or add a piece of meat as well.

6 pounds beef bones and/or knuckles

3 carrots, cut into 2-inch pieces

3 celery stalks, cut into 2-inch pieces

2 onions, skins on, quartered

4 ounces tomato paste

2 cups plus 4 quarts cold water

¼ teaspoon dried thyme

½ teaspoon dried rosemary

1 bay leaf

12 peppercorns

Cheesecloth

Preheat the oven to 400°F. Place the beef bones, carrots, celery, onions and tomato paste in a large roasting pan. Toss to coat the bones and vegetables in the paste. Place in the oven and roast for 1 hour, stirring every 20 minutes.

When the bones have browned, remove them from the roasting pan and place in a large stock pot. Deglaze the pan by placing it over a burner set on high heat and adding 2 cups of water. Scrape any of the browned bits off the bottom of the pan and pour the liquid into the pot with the bones. Add enough cold water to cover the bones, about 4 quarts, and bring to a boil over high heat. Wrap the herbs in the cheesecloth, tie with a cotton string and place in the pot. Lower the heat until the stock simmers and cook for 6 hours. Remove from the heat and strain through a cheesecloth placed in a fine-meshed sieve. Allow to cool completely before refrigerating or freezing.

Chicken Stock

EVERY GOOD COOK HAS their own tried and true method of making chicken stock, one of the essentials in a culinary repertoire. It's the foundation of many soups and stews, so that balancing the seasonings and the savory vegetables that enhance the rich chicken flavor is a coveted skill. But like any skill, it's one that can be learned. I'm sharing my method here with the simple trick of studding an onion with a few whole cloves, a secret ingredient I learned from my mother that adds a subtle flavor.

3 pounds chicken parts (such as wings, necks, backs)

1 bay leaf

½ teaspoon dried thyme

12 peppercorns

2 celery stalks, coarsely chopped

1 large onion, stuck with 3 cloves

2 carrots, coarsely chopped

6 parsley sprigs

12 cups cold water

Place all of the ingredients in a large pot. Bring to a boil, and reduce the heat until the stock simmers gently. Cook for 2 hours, do not stir. Skim the gray foam off the surface as it rises. Remove from the heat. Place a sieve lined with cheesecloth over a large bowl. Carefully strain the stock through the sieve. Discard the solid matter.

Be sure to allow the stock to cool completely before storing in plastic containers in the refrigerator or freezer.

Fish Stock

MAKES 1 QUART

LIKE ANY STOCK, THIS ONE WILL add a depth of flavor to a dish that surpasses water or other liquid. While this recipe calls for the bones and heads from white-fleshed fish, a stock made from lobster or shrimp shells is also outstanding and highly recommended should the ingredients be available. It's best to avoid using oily fish like salmon or mackerel as they will make the stock too oily and fishy.

3 pounds bones and heads from white fleshed fish

2 onions, thinly sliced

1 bunch parsley

2 teaspoons fresh lemon juice

½ cup mushroom trimmings

2 cups dry white wine

1 quart cold water

Cheesecloth

Place all of the ingredients in a large stock pot and bring to a boil over high heat. Lower the heat until the stock barely simmers and cook for 45 minutes. Remove from the heat and strain through cheesecloth placed in a fine meshed sieve. Cool completely before refrigerating or freezing.

Vegetable Stock

MAKES 2 QUARTS

WHILE THE FLAVOR INTENSITY OF an all vegetable stock will always be milder than beef or chicken stock, it still has many uses, not the least of which is satisfying vegetarian preferences when making a soup or stew. Remember that the higher the proportion of vegetables to water, the more flavorful the stock. Improvise and use a selection of mature seasonal vegetables or the reliable ones listed here, but do not over-cook them or the stock's delicate flavor will be lost.

3	onions, peeled, quartered
4	carrots, cut into 2-inch pieces
2	celery stalks, cut into 2-inch pieces
1	leek, rinsed well, cut into 2-inch pieces
1	bunch parsley
10	peppercorns
1	cup mushrooms, halved
2	cloves garlic, crushed
2½	quarts cold water
	Cheesecloth

Place first nine ingredients in a large pot and cover with cold water. Bring to a boil over high heat. Lower the heat until the stock simmers and cook for 30 minutes. Strain through cheesecloth placed in a fine-meshed sieve. Cool completely before refrigerating or freezing.

STEWS

Classic Beef Stew	Oregon Spring Stew
Beef and Pork Picado	Lamb Korma
Beef and Oats Stew	Navarin D'Agneau
After Church Stew	Andouille and Chicken Jambalaya
Beef in Guinness	Hoppin' John
New England Boiled Dinner	Pork Pot Stew
Guisado de Picadillo	Pork and Vegetable Goulash
Spring Stew with Vegetables	Couscous Tajine.
Beef and Sausage Goulash	Oregonian Turkey Chili
Asian Beef	Chicken Creole
Lamb and Barley Stew	Chicken Vindaloo

Coq au Vin

Pollo en Pina

Chicken Fricassee

Country Captain Chicken

Spicy Turkey Stew

Brunswick Stew

Indian Chickpea Stew

Corn, Squash and
Green Chili Stew

Spicy Red Bean Stew

Spinach, Potato and Lentil Stew

Autumn Vegetable Stew

Caribbean Fish and
Sausage Stew

Desert Island Tuna

Clam and Corn Stew

Italian Salmon Stew

Fisher's Island Stew

'Sconset Stew

Shrimp Etouffée

Grouper Creole

Classic Beef Stew

SERVES 6

PRACTICAL, AS WELL AS DELICIOUS, the beauty of a robust stew like this one is that it can be prepared in advance during the day and served as a full meal in the evening. The slow, steady simmering tenderizes the meat and also frees a cook to leave the kitchen if necessary. My interpretation of a classic beef stew, this recipe calls for red wine, dried thyme, all-spice and Worcestershire sauce, seasonings that add sophisticated flavor to the beef.

1	pound new potatoes, peeled, quartered
2	pounds beef top round
1	large onion, sliced
3	carrots, peeled, cut into 2-inch pieces
2	cloves garlic, minced
½	pound mushrooms, quartered
1	14-ounce can tomatoes with their juices, chopped
¼	cup dry red wine
2	cups beef broth
2	teaspoons Worcestershire sauce
1	bay leaf
½	teaspoon dried thyme
¼	teaspoon ground allspice
1	cup fresh or frozen peas

Place all of the ingredients in a large, heavy pot and bring to a boil over high heat. Lower the heat until the stew simmers. Cover and cook for 2 to 2½ hours, until the beef is very tender.

Serve with toasted English muffins.

67

Beef and Pork Picado

SERVES 6 TO 8

My adaptation of this traditional Portuguese stew includes pork and jalapeño peppers. A hearty dish with a tantalizing fragrance of garlic and tomatoes, it's one that I think will quickly become a family favorite. To streamline preparation, purchase beef pre-cut for kebabs and stews. Just before serving, ladle the juice remaining in the stockpot over the meat to fully enjoy the rich blend of Mediterranean flavors.

2 pounds beef chuck, cut into 1½-inch cubes

1½ pounds pork butt, cut into 1½-inch cubes

2 onions, cut into wedges

2 green bell peppers, seeded, chopped

2 cups beef broth

4 tomatoes, cut into wedges

4 cloves garlic, minced

1 fresh or pickled jalapeno pepper, minced

¼ teaspoon freshly ground pepper

½ teaspoon salt

Place the meat in a 5- to 6-quart pot, cover and cook over medium heat for 10 minutes. Uncover and cook for another 5 minutes, stirring occasionally, until the juices have evaporated. Add the onions and peppers and cook for another 5 minutes. Add the remaining ingredients and bring to a simmer. Reduce the heat, cover and cook for about 2½ hours, until the meat is very tender. Uncover and simmer until the juices reduce to just cover the meat and the stew is thickened.

Serve with corn bread (see recipe on page 122).

Beef and Oats Stew

SERVES 6

MANY PEASANT FAMILIES LIVING in rural Ireland or Wales added rolled oats or oatmeal to meat stews to thicken and extend them so they would serve more people. Here a small measure of oats adds texture and helps to thicken the stew. I like to use thick cut or country-style bacon in this recipe to boost its flavor. For best results, use "old-fashioned" or steel cut oats, not instant oatmeal.

2 strips bacon, chopped

1½ pounds beef top round, cut into 2-inch cubes

2 large onions, sliced

3 carrots, sliced

3 parsnips, sliced

2 celery stalks, diced

⅓ cup rolled oats

2 quarts water

3 potatoes, peeled, diced

Preheat the oven to 350°F.

In a large, heavy skillet, over medium-high heat, sauté the bacon until the fat is rendered, about 5 minutes. Add the beef and cook in the bacon fat until it is browned on all sides, about 10 minutes. Add the onions, carrots, parsnips and celery and sauté for another 7 minutes. Place into an ovenproof pot and add the oats and water. Bring to a boil, cover and place in the oven. Cook for 2 hours. Add the potatoes and cook for another hour.

Serve with buttered egg noodles.

After Church Stew

SERVES 6

Yes, church ladies are practical as well as devout. This stew is designed to be almost ready-to-eat when everyone comes home from Sunday services. It's an old-fashioned recipe, probably from the Midwest, and it combines tried and true stew ingredients like chuck steak, potatoes, carrots, celery and tomatoes in one generous stockpot. Simply place all ingredients together in the pot except the potatoes and set the timer for three hours later. Add the potatoes and when they're cooked, you're ready to eat.

1 ½	pounds chuck steak, cut into 1-inch cubes
2	teaspoons salt
½	teaspoon dried basil
½	teaspoon freshly ground pepper
2	stalks celery, cut into diagonal slices
4	carrots, cut into diagonal slices
2	onions, cut into ½-inch slices
1	16-ounce can crushed tomatoes
3	potatoes, peeled, cut into ¾-inch cubes

Preheat the oven to 300°F.

Place all ingredients except the potatoes in a 3- to 5-quart oven-safe casserole and toss well. Cover and place in the oven for 3 hours. Add the potatoes and cook for another 45 minutes.

Serve with warm Italian bread.

Beef in Guinness

SERVES 6

As terrific as it is for drinking, Guinness Stout from Ireland is one of the very best beers to cook with and is often the "secret ingredient" of many dishes. In this recipe, the alcohol in the hearty, dark Irish brew cooks away, while the beer imparts a subtle flavor to the cubed beef and vegetables with their fragrant juices seasoned by orange rind, mustard and tomato paste.

2   pounds top round of beef, cut into 1-inch cubes

½   cup flour

⅓   cup corn oil

1   large onion, sliced

1   carrot, sliced

2   stalks celery, sliced

1   teaspoon dry mustard

1   teaspoon tomato paste

1   1 x 3-inch strip of orange rind, pith removed

2½   cups Guinness

Salt and freshly ground pepper to taste

Toss the beef in the flour to coat. Heat half the oil in a large, deep pot, over high heat, and cook the beef until browned on all sides, about 10 minutes. Remove from the pan and set aside. Add the remaining oil, lower the heat to medium, and sauté the onions until they brown, about 5 minutes. Add the carrot and celery and cook for another 2 to 3 minutes. Stir in the mustard, tomato paste, orange rind, and Guinness. Raise the heat and bring the stew to a boil. Return the beef and any juices to the pot and simmer for 2 to 2½ hours. Add water if necessary to keep the beef covered. Adjust the seasoning with salt and pepper to taste.

Serve over egg noodles.

New England Boiled Dinner

SERVES 6 TO 8

BOILING FRESH MEAT WAS COMMON in 19th century New England, especially during winter when kitchen fires burned all day and provided the steady heat necessary for boiling. Assorted winter vegetables that could be stored successfully were also available to inspire a cook and add to the stew pot, so it's not surprising that this dish became a New England standard. When winter winds blow, it's still one of the most satisfying main dishes around.

3	pounds corned beef
2	quarts water
3	whole cloves
1	bay leaf
1	teaspoon freshly ground pepper
1	large, yellow turnip, peeled, diced
½	head cabbage, quartered
4	large carrots, cut into 1-inch pieces
4	large potatoes, peeled, quartered
1	15-ounce can beets, drained, sliced
2	tablespoons butter
	Salt to taste

Place the corned beef in a large, heavy pot and cover with the water. Bring to a boil, add the cloves, bay leaf and pepper, lower the heat to a simmer, and cook for 3 hours. Add the turnips and cabbage and cook for another ½ hour. Add the carrots and potatoes and cook for ½ hour.

In a heavy skillet over medium-high heat, sauté the beets in the butter until they are heated through, about 5 minutes. Adjust the seasoning with salt to taste.

Lift the meat and vegetables out of the pot, remove the cloves and bay leaf, and place on a large platter. Thinly slice the beef. Surround with the beets.

Serve with corn bread sticks.

Guisado de Picadillo

SERVES 6

Another culinary crossroads in America, the Southwest, shows the influence of Spain in this recipe. Borrowing its name from a Spanish cooking term, this spicy stew combines sautéed strips of thinly sliced meat, or picadillo, *with Southwestern ingredients such as tomatillos and zucchini. Potatoes are another New World addition. Simmered in a cumin-flavored red chili sauce, this is a satisfying main dish, especially when with served with rice and refried beans.*

- 1 pound fresh tomatillos or 13 ounces canned
- 2 tablespoons corn oil
- 2 pounds boneless top round beef, thinly sliced across the grain
- 1 teaspoon cumin seeds
- 1 pound red potatoes, thinly sliced
- 1 pound zucchini, ends trimmed, sliced ¼-inch thick
- 1 10-ounce can red chili sauce
- 4 cups hot cooked rice
- 1 large, ripe avocado, peeled, pitted, sliced
- Chopped fresh cilantro for garnish
- Sour cream for garnish

Pull off and discard husks and stems from fresh tomatillos. Rinse well and slice ¼-inch thick.

Pour the oil into a large, deep skillet and place over a medium-high heat. Add the beef and cumin seeds and cook, stirring occasionally, until the beef is no longer pink, about 5 to 7 minutes. Add tomatillos (if using canned, include the liquid), potatoes, zucchini and chili sauce. Bring to a boil. Reduce the heat, cover and simmer until the potatoes are soft, about 30 minutes.

Spoon the stew over rice, surround with avocado, sprinkle with cilantro and top with a dollop of sour cream.

Accompany with bowls of salsa, refried beans, guacamole and flour tortillas.

Spring Stew with Vegetables

SERVES 6 TO 8

A STEW FEATURING LAMB AND BEEF with fresh vegetables and barley is a classic combination in many countries. To make this satisfying main dish, seek out the first new peas and beans from the garden or farmer's market if you're not growing your own in the backyard. Braising the meat first seals in juices, while pearl barley offers wholesome, delicate texture. Be sure to add tender vegetables like peas last so they won't become overcooked.

2 tablespoons olive oil

1 pound lamb shoulder, cut into 1-inch cubes

1 pound top round of beef, cut into 1-inch cubes

2 carrots, peeled, sliced

1 onion, chopped

1 pound turnips, peeled, diced

½ cup barley, rinsed

3 cups hot beef broth

½ teaspoon freshly ground pepper

½ pound green beans, cut into 1-inch pieces

½ pound fresh or frozen peas

Preheat the oven to 325°F.

Heat the oil in a 5- to 6-quart ovenproof pot over high heat. Add the lamb and beef and cook, stirring often, until the meat is browned, about 7 to 10 minutes. Remove from the pot and keep warm. Reduce the heat to medium and add the carrots, onion, and turnips and cook until the onion is limp, about 5 minutes. Return the meat to the pot. Add the barley, broth and pepper. Bring to a boil over high heat, cover and place in the oven. Cook for 1½ to 2 hours, until the meat is tender. Stir in the beans and peas and cook for another 15 minutes.

Serve with buttermilk biscuits (see recipe on page 124).

Beef and Sausage Goulash

SERVES 6 TO 8

HUNGARY'S MOST NOTABLE CONTRIBUTION to the culinary world is paprika or dried red pepper. The brilliant red spice took the country's cooks by storm in the early 1800's by adding appealing color, taste and fragrance to many native dishes. This classic version of the Hungarian stew named "porkolt," which Americans call "goulash," includes a generous measure of paprika as well as other typical ingredients like cubed beef, sausage, onions, beef broth and selected seasonings.

1½ cups chopped onion

1 green bell pepper, seeded, chopped

1 pound hot or spicy sausage links, cut into ½-inch slices

⅓ cup flour

2 tablespoons Hungarian sweet paprika

2 pounds beef chuck, cut into 1-inch cubes

2 teaspoons red wine vinegar

3 cups beef broth

1 teaspoon salt

In a deep, heavy pot, sauté the onions, green pepper, and sausage over low heat until the vegetables are soft and the fat is rendered.

In a medium-sized bowl, combine the paprika and flour. Dredge the meat in the flour and add to the vegetables and sausage. Reserve any left over flour mixture. Turn the heat to high and cook the beef until it begins to brown. Add any leftover flour, the red wine vinegar and beef broth. Bring to a boil and then lower the heat until the stew simmers. Cook for 2 hours, stirring occasionally. Stir in the salt.

Serve with mashed potatoes.

Asian Beef

SERVES 6

SO MANY ASIAN FLAVORS and ingredients are now familiar to Americans as immigrants from this part of the world have introduced us to ethnic cuisines from Thailand, Vietnam, Indonesia and other countries in Southeast Asia. Not surprisingly, given the appeal of the one-dish meal to cooks everywhere, Asian cuisines also include stews. I've adapted one of my favorites in this recipe featuring strips of beef browned in peanut oil and infused with a fragrant mixture of soy sauce, rice vinegar, fresh ginger and zesty red pepper flakes.

- 2 pounds beef chuck, cut into 1½-inch strips
- 3 tablespoons peanut oil
- 1½ cup chicken broth
- ¼ cup soy sauce
- 2 tablespoons rice vinegar
- 3 thin slices gingerroot
- 3 scallions, thinly sliced, cut into 2-inch strips
- 1 tablespoon sugar
- ¼ teaspoon red pepper flakes
- 2 tablespoons toasted sesame seeds
- 2 tablespoons chopped fresh cilantro

Brown the beef in the peanut oil in a wok over high heat, about 7 to 10 minutes. Add the broth, soy sauce, vinegar, ginger, scallions, sugar, and red pepper flakes. Bring to a boil, cover and lower the heat to a simmer and cook for 1 hour, until the beef is tender. Before serving, sprinkle with sesame seeds and cilantro.

Serve with rice or Asian noodles.

Lamb and Barley Stew

SERVES 6

One of the ancient grains of the kitchen, with its use dating to Greek and Roman times when it was a staple food all around the Mediterranean, barley is still a favorite among cooks. It sailed to the New World with European settlers and today is primarily a crop raised for cattle fodder. Pearl barley, with the outer bran husk polished off, is the form used most often in soups and stews. It is paired here with boneless lamb chunks for a delicious, satisfying result.

2	tablespoons unsalted butter
3	carrots, chopped
2	large celery stalks, chopped
2	onions, chopped
3	garlic cloves, minced
1½	cups pearl barley, rinsed
5	cups beef broth
2½	pounds lean, boneless lamb, cut into ½-inch pieces
	Salt and freshly ground pepper to taste

Melt the butter in a large, heavy pot, over medium-high heat. Add the carrots, celery, onion and garlic and sauté until the onions are soft, about 10 minutes. Add the barley and stir until it's mixed in. Add the broth and lamb. Raise the heat until the stew comes to a boil. Lower the heat, cover and simmer until the lamb is cooked, about 45 to 60 minutes. Adjust the seasoning with salt and pepper.

Serve with toasted English muffins.

Oregon Spring Stew

SERVES 6

WHEN THE SEASONS TURN FROM WINTER to spring, I always appreciate a change from hardy root vegetables to the first fresh green ones. At the same time, first spring lamb arrives in the markets, so it's an appropriate time to celebrate the change of season with a spring stew. Lamb, along with green beans and peas, plus other vegetables and beef, makes this an especially hearty stew for those evenings when the weather hasn't decided yet if it's spring or still winter.

Heat the oil in a large pot over high heat. Add the lamb and beef and cook, stirring, until browned, about 10 minutes. Remove from the pot and set aside. Add the carrots, onions and turnips. Cook, stirring often, until onion is limp, about 5 to 7 minutes. Return the meat to the pot and add the brown rice, broth, pepper and enough water to completely cover the meat and vegetables. Bring to a boil over high heat. Lower the heat and cover. Simmer for 1 hour. Stir in the green beans and peas.

Serve with poppy seed muffins.

1 tablespoon corn oil

1 pound lean, boneless lamb, cut into 1-inch cubes

1 pound top round beef, cut into 1-inch cubes

3 carrots, thinly sliced

1 large onion, chopped

1 small turnip, peeled, diced

½ cup brown rice

4 cups beef broth

1 to 2 cups water

½ teaspoon freshly ground pepper

½ pound green beans, trimmed, cut into 1-inch pieces

1 cup fresh or frozen peas

Lamb Korma

SERVES 6 TO 8

DRAW AN ARCH STRETCHING FROM Syria and Lebanon through Turkey, all the way to Afghanistan, Pakistan and India, and korma appears on menus in every country. While variations of the dish are found in each region, the generic culinary term generally refers to meat braised on a stovetop or meat cooked slowly like a stew, to which herbs and spices are added. This version, with a small amount of liquid and yogurt, curry, chili powder and other pungent spices in the thick sauce, is closest to an Indian korma.

1 large onion, sliced into rings

3 tablespoons corn oil

1 cinnamon stick

6 whole cloves

½ teaspoon cardamom seeds

1 bay leaf

1 teaspoon cumin seeds

2 tablespoons grated gingerroot

2 cloves garlic, minced

2 pounds lamb shoulder, cut into 1-inch cubes

1 teaspoon chili powder

1 tablespoon curry powder

½ cup plain yogurt

½ cup water

½ teaspoon salt

2 tablespoons slivered almonds

1 tablespoon chopped fresh cilantro

In a deep skillet, sauté the onion in the oil over medium heat for 5 to 7 minutes, until golden brown. Add the cinnamon, cloves, cardamom, bay leaf and cumin and cook for 1 minute. Add the ginger, garlic and lamb cubes. Sprinkle with the chili and curry powder. Mix well and cook for 5 minutes. Add the yogurt, water and salt. Cover and simmer for 45 minutes.

Crush the almonds with a rolling pin until they are powdery. Just before serving, stir in the almonds and cilantro.

Serve with pita bread.

Navarin d'Agneau

SERVES 6

THE FRENCH WORD FOR "TURNIP" is navet *which is probably the source of the cooking term "navarin." In France, the stew with this name is made with lamb and typically features seasonal vegetables. During winter months, potatoes and onions are used, while in spring and early summer the first new vegetables from the garden—peas, carrots, beans and turnips—combine with chunks of succulent lamb in a savory broth flavored with herbs.*

2   pounds lamb shoulder, cut into 1-inch cubes

¼   cup olive oil

4   onions, sliced

4   carrots, peeled, sliced

1   white turnip, peeled, diced

¼   cup flour

3   cups chicken broth

Bouquet garni (purchased or substitute 1 teaspoon each: thyme, parsley, rosemary, tarragon, and 1 bayleaf wrapped in cheesecloth)

1   tablespoon tomato paste

1   clove garlic, crushed

Salt and freshly ground pepper to taste

In a deep skillet, brown the lamb over medium heat in the oil, about 7 to 10 minutes. Add the vegetables and flour, and sauté for 5 to 7 minutes, stirring often. Add the broth, bouquet garni, tomato paste and garlic. Bring to a boil. Lower the heat to a simmer, cover and cook for 1½ to 2 hours, until the meat is very tender. Season with salt and pepper.

Serve with warm French bread.

Andouille and Chicken Jambalaya

SERVES 6

STROLL THE STREETS OF NEW ORLEANS at dinnertime as I have and your nose will lead you to a dozen restaurants where jambalaya is simmering. Inspired by Spanish paella, jambalaya is New Orleans' signature dish. It can be made with any combination of various ingredients including chicken, sausage, prawns, oysters, peppers, and tomatoes. In this version, andouille sausage, named for the region in France where it originated, and chicken compliment each other well.

⅓ cup corn oil

2½ cups chopped onion

1 cup chopped green peppers

2 teaspoons salt

1 teaspoon cayenne pepper

¾ pound andouille sausage, cut into ¼-inch slices

1 pound boneless chicken meat (use both white and dark), cut into 1-inch cubes

2 bay leaves

3 cups white rice

6 cups water

1 cup chopped scallions

Heat the oil in a large, heavy pot over medium heat. Add the onions, green peppers, 1 teaspoon salt and cayenne. Stirring often, sauté the vegetables until they are dark brown in color, about 20 minutes. Add the sausage and cook for 10 to 15 minutes, scraping to loosen any browned bits.

Season the chicken with 1 teaspoon salt. Add the chicken and bay leaves to the pot and brown for 8 to 10 minutes. Add the rice and water and stir well. Bring to a boil, then lower the heat, cover and simmer for 30 to 35 minutes. Remove from the heat and let sit, covered, for 3 minutes. Remove the bay leaves and stir in the scallions.

Serve with hush puppies (see recipe on page 125).

Hoppin' John

SERVES 4 TO 6

THIS IS ONE OF THE MORE CURIOUS stews to make its way into American culinary traditions. A variation of the many rice and bean dishes in Southern cooking, it called for a base of cowpeas, or black-eyed peas, cooked with fat pork, rice and seasonings. This updated version uses ham, but is every bit as good. While the origin of the name of the dish is uncertain, most culinary historians agree that the stew has roots in African cooking traditions.

3 cups chicken broth

2 tomatoes, chopped

10 scallions, chopped

1 bay leaf

1 teaspoon dried thyme

1 teaspoon hot sauce (such as Tabasco)

1½ cups white rice

1 16-ounce can of black-eyed peas, drained, rinsed

1 pound cooked ham, cut into ½-inch cubes

In a 5- to 6-quart pot, bring the broth, tomatoes, scallions, bay leaf, thyme and hot sauce to a boil over high heat. Add the rice, cover and lower the heat to a simmer. Cook for 15 minutes. Stir in the black-eyed peas and ham. Cook for another 5 minutes.

Serve with hush puppies (see recipe on page 125).

Pork Pot Stew

SERVES 6 TO 8

ALMOST EVERY COUNTRY HAS sausages in its culinary repertoire, since sausages are one of the world's oldest foods, dating at least to Greek and Roman times, if not earlier. Sausages can be made from fish, fowl or meat, and were a convenient way to use up every scrap of an animal after butchering. For this stew, assorted sausages from Italy and Poland are browned and simmered with cubes of tender pork loin in a hearty sauce of baked beans and tomatoes. Adding a dash of bourbon gives this stew a novel flavor.

1 pound hot Italian sausage links, cut into 1-inch pieces

1 pound kielbasa, cut into 1-inch pieces

2 onions, diced

2 tablespoons corn oil

1 pound pork loin, cut into 1-inch cubes

2 15.5-ounce cans baked beans

1 14-ounce can crushed tomatoes with their juices

⅓ cup bourbon

In a large, heavy pot, cook the Italian sausage, kielbasa, and onions in the corn oil over medium heat until browned, about 10 minutes. Add the pork and brown on all sides for 5 to 7 minutes. Stir in the remaining ingredients, except the bourbon and simmer for 1 hour. Add water if needed. Five minutes before serving, mix in the bourbon and simmer for 5 minutes.

Serve with potato pancakes.

Pork and Vegetable Goulash

SERVES 6 TO 8

In Hungary, the word "goulash" means cattle driver, or "cowboy." Since the 9th century, Hungarian cattlemen, sheepherders and pigherders have been eating a dish made from cooked, cubed meat seasoned with onions and spices. Oddly enough, in every other part of the world the word "goulash" is associated with a hearty meat stew seasoned with paprika, a name travelers to Hungary gave to a special dish served to honored guests and visitors. In some parts of the United States, "goulash" is so popular that it's considered a basic American dish.

½ cup flour

1 teaspoon salt

¼ teaspoon freshly ground pepper

2 pounds pork loin, cut into 1-inch cubes

1 tablespoon unsalted butter

3½ cups beef broth

1 onion, chopped

½ cup shredded carrot

¼ cup chopped fresh parsley

½ cup chopped leek

½ cup chopped celery

3 tomatoes, quartered

In a deep, wide bowl, combine the flour, salt and pepper. Dredge the pork in the flour and shake off the excess. In a heavy pot, over medium-high heat, brown the pork in the butter, about 8 to 10 minutes. Add the broth and simmer for 20 minutes. Add the onion, carrot, parsley, leek and celery. Cover and simmer for 30 minutes, or until the vegetables are tender. Add the tomatoes and simmer for 5 to 10 minutes more.

Serve over buttered egg noodles.

Couscous Tajine

SERVES 6

MOROCCO IS FAMOUS FOR its tajines, a word meaning both the savory, or savory and sweet, stews that are an integral part of this exotic North African country's cuisine, as well as the elegant earthenware cooking vessels they are cooked in. Traditionally served over a bed of couscous, tajines typically pair lamb or chicken with assorted vegetables, or sometimes even fruit, in a sauce seasoned by aromatic spices like turmeric, coriander and cayenne pepper.

3	large skinless boneless chicken breasts, halved
2	tablespoons olive oil
3	small carrots, cut into ¼-inch rounds
1	medium onion, sliced
1	pound yellow turnips, diced
2	cloves garlic, minced
2	teaspoons ground coriander
1	teaspoon salt
¼	teaspoon cayenne pepper
¼	teaspoon ground turmeric
1	cup chicken broth
1	small zucchini, cut into ¼-inch rounds
1	cup canned chickpeas, drained, rinsed
1⅓	cups couscous
¾	cup raisins
½	teaspoon salt
1	cup boiling water
⅓	cup butter
½	teaspoon ground turmeric

Brown the chicken in the oil in a deep, heavy skillet, over medium-high heat for about 7 to 10 minutes. Add the carrots, onion, turnip, garlic, coriander, salt, cayenne, and turmeric and sauté for 5 minutes. Add the broth, zucchini and chickpeas. Cover and simmer for 15 to 20 minutes, until the vegetables are tender.

Mix the couscous, raisins and salt in a 2-quart bowl. Stir in the boiling water and cover. Let sit for 5 minutes, until the water is absorbed. Melt the butter in a large skillet and add the turmeric. Add the couscous and cook for 5 minutes.

Place a mound of couscous on each plate and place half a chicken breast, sauce and vegetables on top.

Serve with pita bread.

Oregonian Turkey Chili

SERVES 6

FROM THE RAINY WOODS OF OREGON comes this innovative chili that looks like chili and tastes like chili, and will warm you to the bottom of your toes just like chili. But there the similarities end. Instead of beef there's ground turkey. Instead of white, black or navy beans, this recipe calls for red kidney beans and other zesty ingredients and seasonings like green pepper, garlic, tomatoes, Cajun pepper and paprika.

- 1 large onion, finely chopped
- 2 tablespoons corn oil
- ½ cup chopped green pepper
- 1 clove garlic, minced
- 1 pound ground turkey, crumbled
- 8 ounces canned tomatoes with their juices
- 22 ounces canned kidney beans, drained
- 15 ounces canned tomato sauce
- 2 tablespoons soy sauce
- 1½ tablespoons chili powder
- ½ teaspoon ground cumin
- ½ teaspoon sage
- ½ teaspoon thyme

Set aside ¼ cup of onion for garnish.

Heat the oil in a 3- to 4-quart heavy pot, over medium-high heat. Add the onions, green pepper and garlic. Sauté, stirring often, until the onions are soft, about 5 minutes. Increase the heat to high and add the turkey and cook, stirring gently, until it begins to brown. Add the remaining ingredients. Stir to remove the browned bits and simmer for 30 minutes. Before serving, sprinkle with the reserved onions. Serve with corn bread sticks.

Chicken Creole

SERVES 6

CHICKEN IS A WONDERFULLY VERSATILE ingredient, adapting to almost any herb or vegetable. It shows off its star power in this recipe with tender and moist chicken breasts in a savory sauce of tomatoes, garlic, onions and green bell peppers. This dish is a fast and easy way to dress up simple chicken for a midweek meal or when guests unexpectedly arrive for dinner.

⅓ corn oil

2 cups diced onions

3 cloves garlic, minced

1½ cups chopped green bell pepper

1 28-ounce can tomatoes with their juices, chopped

1 bay leaf

1 teaspoon dried thyme

½ teaspoon freshly ground pepper

3 skinless boneless chicken breasts, halved

¼ cup chopped fresh parsley

In a heavy, deep skillet, heat the oil over medium heat. Add the onions and garlic and sauté for 5 to 7 minutes. Add the remaining ingredients, except for the parsley, being sure to cover the chicken with the sauce. Simmer the stew for ½ hour. Just before serving, sprinkle with the parsley.

Serve over rice.

Chicken Vindaloo

SERVES 6

INDIAN RESTAURANTS AROUND *the world feature "vindaloo" among their curry selections. While many people think the term means the hottest curry available, that's incorrect. The name actually refers to seasonings of garlic and wine vinegar in a Portuguese pork stew once common in Goa, a city on the West Coast of India that was formerly a colony of Portugal. Innovative native cooks in Goa adapted the dish and added ingredients like ginger, cumin, cardamom and hot pepper.*

⅓ cup white wine vinegar

6 cloves garlic, peeled

3 tablespoons peeled, chopped gingerroot

1 tablespoon curry powder

2 teaspoons ground cumin

1 teaspoon ground cardamom

½ teaspoon cayenne pepper

2½ pounds skinless boneless chicken thigh, cubed

⅓ cup olive oil

3 cups chopped onions

1 14-ounce can tomatoes with their juices, chopped

1 cinnamon stick

½ cup chopped fresh cilantro

Place the first 7 ingredients in a blender or a food processor and puree into a paste. Scrape into a medium-size bowl and add the chicken cubes. Toss to coat.

Place the olive oil and onions in a large, heavy pot over medium-high heat and cook for 7 to 10 minutes, until they begin to brown. Add the chicken and cook for 3 to 5 minutes. Add the tomatoes, and cinnamon and bring to a boil. Reduce the heat, cover and simmer until the chicken is tender, about ½ hour. Stir in the cilantro.

Serve over rice with mango chutney.

Coq-au-Vin

SERVES 6

NOT SO LONG AGO, IT WAS COMMON for French families living in the countryside to keep chickens and a rooster—or coq—to supply the household with eggs and fresh poultry. When a rooster's breeding years were over, he became dinner. Because of their age, cocks needed long, slow cooking in a casserole to become tender. Hence enterprising French cooks created "coq au vin." While chicken is used today to make this classic dish—generally young chickens require a shorter cooking time—the method of browning the pieces, setting them ablaze under a glaze of brandy, and simmering them in a wine sauce fragrant with herbs, closely follows French tradition.

3	pounds skinless boneless chicken breast
5	tablespoons unsalted butter, divided
4	shallots, chopped
4	slices bacon, chopped
⅓	cup brandy
1	cup red wine
1½	cups chicken broth
½	teaspoon salt
1	teaspoon freshly ground pepper
1	teaspoon dried thyme
½	teaspoon dried tarragon
1	clove garlic, minced
4	ounces button mushrooms
⅓	cup flour

Melt 3 tablespoons of the butter in a deep, heavy skillet, over medium-high heat. Add the chicken and cook until browned. Remove and keep warm. Add the shallots and bacon and cook for 5 minutes, until the shallots are lightly browned. Return the chicken to the skillet and add the brandy. Ignite and shake the pan until the flames extinguish. Add the wine, broth, salt, pepper, thyme, tarragon, garlic and mushrooms. Bring to a boil, cover, reduce the heat and simmer until the chicken is tender, about 20 to 25 minutes.

Remove the chicken and keep warm. In a small bowl, mix the flour with the remaining 2 tablespoons of butter. Bring the cooking liquid to a boil and add the flour paste, a little at a time, and stir until the sauce is thickened. Return the chicken to the pot and serve very hot.

Serve with parslied potatoes.

Pollo en Pina

SERVES 6

FAMILY COOKS ARE OFTEN KNOWN by the recipes they keep. In this instance, my aunt's chicken and pineapple stew was one of the most sought-after recipes in our family. While she never quite got around to writing it down, I did take notes one time while she named the ingredients and spices. I've interpreted her recipe here and I think its sweet-savory flavors with the hints of cinnamon and cloves make it every bit as delicious as her original. I think she'd agree.

2 tablespoons olive oil

3 pounds skinless boneless chicken breast, cut into 2-inch cubes

1 onion, chopped

1 16-ounce can unsweetened pineapple chunks, drained

½ cup dry sherry

2 tablespoons white wine vinegar

1 teaspoon salt

¼ teaspoon ground cinnamon

¼ teaspoon ground cloves

¼ teaspoon freshly ground pepper

2 large tomatoes, coarsely chopped

Heat the olive oil in a large, deep skillet over medium heat. Add the chicken and sauté until the chicken is browned, about 10 minutes. Remove the chicken and add the onion. Sauté until it is tender, about 5 to 7 minutes. Return the chicken to the skillet and add the remaining ingredients and simmer for 20 minutes.

Serve over rice.

Chicken Fricassee

THIS CLASSIC FRENCH DISH where chicken pieces are first browned in a skillet, then simmered in broth, and finally served under a luscious, buttery white sauce belies its humble origins in 17th century France. Back then, fricassée was considered a rather common cooking method. It's now an elegant way to prepare plain chicken and we're all the luckier. The dish is always a favorite at my house when we're having guests for an informal Sunday night supper.

3	pounds chicken parts, separated at the joint
¼	cup olive oil
1	large onion, stuck with 10 whole cloves
1	large carrot, cut into 1-inch pieces
1	stalk celery, cut into 1-inch pieces
½	teaspoon dried thyme
1	bay leaf
¼	teaspoon dried tarragon
1	teaspoon salt
3	cups chicken broth
3	tablespoons butter
¼	cup flour
1	egg yolk
½	cup milk
1	teaspoon lemon juice
1	tablespoon chopped fresh parsley

In a large, heavy pot, over medium-high heat, brown the chicken in the olive oil, about 7 to 10 minutes. Add the vegetables, herbs and 3 cups of chicken broth. Raise the heat, cover and simmer for 30 minutes.

Strain off the broth and reserve 2 cups for the sauce. Cover and set aside the chicken and vegetables. In a large, heavy skillet, over medium heat, melt the butter and stir in the flour. Cook for 3 minutes. Slowly pour in the broth and whisk until blended and thickened. Simmer for 5 minutes. In a small bowl, whisk together the egg yolk and milk. Pour about ½ cup of the hot sauce into the egg mixture and then gradually add the mixture back into the sauce. Turn the heat off and whisk in the lemon juice to blend well. Pour the sauce over the chicken and vegetables, and sprinkle with the parsley.

Serve over rice.

Country Captain Chicken

SERVES 6

SEAFARERS AND LANDLUBBERS ALIKE will enjoy this robust chicken stew with its intriguing Indian influences. The subtle flavor of curry, plus currants and herb seasonings in the tomato-green pepper sauce, make this a favorite chicken dish at my house. Served in a festive ring of rice sprinkled with crunchy toasted almonds, it's sophisticated enough for a dinner party. It's also easy to prepare in advance.

3 pounds skinless boneless chicken breast

½ cup flour

⅓ cup corn oil

1 medium onion, chopped

1 medium green pepper, seeded, chopped

1 clove garlic, crushed

Pinch of salt and freshly ground pepper

2 teaspoon curry powder

32 ounces canned tomatoes

2 teaspoon chopped fresh parsley

¼ teaspoon dried marjoram

4 tablespoons currants

4 ounces blanched almond halves

3 cups cooked rice

½ cup cooked corn kernels

2 tablespoons chopped fresh parsley

Preheat the oven to 350°F.

Coat the chicken with the flour and shake off any excess. In a deep, heavy skillet, heat the oil and brown the chicken over medium-high heat. Remove from the pan and place in an ovenproof casserole.

Add the onion, pepper and garlic to the skillet and sauté over medium heat until soft, about 5 minutes. Add the salt, pepper and curry powder and cook for another 3 minutes. Add the tomatoes, parsley, and marjoram. Bring to a boil over high heat. Pour the sauce over the chicken in the casserole. Cover and place in the oven for 45 minutes. Add the currants during the last 15 minutes of the cooking time.

While the stew is cooking, place the almonds on a cookie sheet and place in the oven until they are toasted. Remove when they begin to brown and place in a bowl to cool.

Toss the rice, corn and parsley together and form into desired shape. Ladle the stew onto the plate and sprinkle with the almonds.

Accompany with mango chutney.

Spicy Turkey Stew

THERE ARE SEVERAL SURPRISES in this delicious stew and horseradish is only one of them. I developed the recipe after contemplating a kitchen filled with leftovers following a Thanksgiving feast. It's a terrific alternative to days and nights of eating turkey sandwiches, which I confess I also love. But enough is enough. Increase the amount of horseradish if you enjoy a spicier stew, and don't forget to stir in the cloves or cranberry sauce!

2   onions, diced

2   carrots, sliced

3   tablespoons unsalted butter

4   pounds skinless boneless turkey breast
    or tenders

½   cup flour

1   teaspoon salt

1   teaspoon freshly ground pepper

½   cup freshly grated or bottled
    horseradish

1   cup whole cranberry sauce

4   whole cloves

3   cups chicken broth

Sauté the onions and carrots in the butter in a large heavy pot, over medium heat, for 5 to 7 minutes. Cut the turkey into 2-inch pieces. Combine the flour, salt and pepper in a large bowl. Dredge the turkey in the flour and add to the vegetables. Add any leftover flour to the pot and cook the meat, turning as each side browns, for about 10 minutes.

Place the remaining ingredients in the pot and bring to a boil over high heat. Lower the heat until the stew simmers and cook for 1 hour.

Serve with buttered egg noodles.

Brunswick Stew

SERVES 6 TO 8

THRIFTY NEW ENGLANDERS especially like the notion of stews where the sum of the parts is always greater than the whole. This savory example stars chicken, a bit of flavorful bacon, plus onions, crushed tomatoes, corn, lima beans and potatoes, and was shared by a good friend's mother who lives in Brunswick, Maine. Hence the stew's name. By using canned and frozen vegetables, this stew can be made year-around. Add the corn and lima beans while still frozen to prevent them from cooking faster than other ingredients in the stew.

2	slices bacon, chopped
1/3	cup flour
1	teaspoon salt
1/2	teaspoon freshly ground pepper
1/4	teaspoon cayenne pepper
3	pounds chicken parts, separated at the joint
3	onions, diced
1	cup canned, crushed tomatoes
10	ounces frozen corn kernels
10	ounces frozen lima beans
1	cup peeled, diced potato
3	cups chicken broth
1	tablespoon Worcestershire sauce

In a deep, heavy pot, over medium heat, cook the bacon until it is crisp and the fat is rendered, about 5 to 7 minutes.

In a large bowl, combine the flour, salt, pepper and cayenne. Dredge the chicken parts in the flour. Increase the heat under the pot to high and add the onions and chicken, turning as each side browns, for 10 minutes. Add the remaining ingredients and bring the stew to a boil. Lower the heat until the stew simmers and cook for 1 hour.

Serve with corn bread (see recipe on page 122).

Indian Chickpea Stew

SERVES 6

ANOTHER ANCIENT LEGUME THAT'S a staple in Indian and Middle Eastern cultures, chickpeas—or garbonzo beans in Spanish cultures—are found in the dishes of countries across North Africa and around the Mediterranean all the way to India. Acclaimed as a highly nutritious ingredient in soups, stews, and purées like hummus and tahini, the small, pale brown beans are pea-shaped and generally sold dried. Look for canned chickpeas to save on cooking time with this hearty vegetarian stew that also features eggplant and tomatoes.

1 large onion, chopped

2 tablespoons olive oil

2 tablespoons curry powder

½ teaspoon ground cumin

Pinch cayenne pepper

3 cloves garlic, minced

3 cups 1-inch cubed eggplant

2 cups peeled, chopped tomatoes

2 cups vegetable broth

2 cups canned chickpeas, drained, rinsed

⅓ cup chopped fresh cilantro

In a deep, heavy skillet, over low heat, sauté the onions in the olive oil until they become clear, about 7 minutes. Add the spices and garlic and continue to cook for another 5 minutes. Add the eggplant and sauté, stirring often, for 7 to 10 minutes, until it begins to brown on all sides. Add the tomatoes, vegetable broth, and chickpeas, raise the heat until it simmers, and cook for 15 minutes. Stir in the cilantro during the last 3 minutes.

Serve over saffron rice.

Corn, Squash and Green Chili Stew

SERVES 6 TO 8

On a trip to Santa Fe a few years ago I was thoroughly hooked by the Southwest's native ingredients like corn, squash, assorted fiery chili peppers and rice. Not only is each delicious on its own, they are also compatible partners in nutritious soups and stews. With that awareness, it wasn't hard to jump into the kitchen and create this zesty stew. Note that fresh, frozen or canned corn can be used depending on the season.

1 tablespoon unsalted butter

1 tablespoon olive oil

1 large onion, diced

½ teaspoon salt

1 cup white rice

2 cups chicken broth or water

2 pounds zucchini, cut into ¾-inch dice

6 ounces green chilies, seeded, diced

½ teaspoon dried marjoram

2 cups fresh or frozen corn kernels

4 ounces Monterey Jack cheese, cut into ½-inch cubes

¼ coarsely chopped fresh parsley

In a 5- to 6-quart pot, over medium heat, melt the butter in the oil. Add the onion and sauté for 5 minutes. Add the salt and rice, stir and sauté for another 3 minutes. Add the chicken broth and bring to a boil. Lower the heat to a simmer and cover. Cook for 10 minutes. Stir in the zucchini, chilies, marjoram and corn kernels, cover and cook for another 10 minutes. Mix in the cheese and parsley and cover until the cheese melts, about 3 to 5 minutes.

Serve with garlic bread (see recipe on page 122).

Spicy Red Bean Stew

SERVES 4 TO 6

THIS RECIPE IS INSPIRED BY Cajun cooking and Louisiana's classic "red beans and rice" dishes. For a long time a version was served by everyone in New Orleans for Monday dinner. The traditional recipe called for cooking the beans at a simmer all day long. This version omits the bacon and sausage, but is still quite spicy. I've also made it quicker and easier to prepare by substituting canned red beans so you don't have to soak the beans overnight.

1 29-ounce can red kidney beans, drained, rinsed

1 14-ounce can crushed tomatoes with their juices

2 red bell peppers, seeded, chopped

2 jalapeño peppers, seeded, diced

2 onions, chopped

2 cloves garlic, minced

2 teaspoons paprika

¼ teaspoon cayenne pepper

Preheat the oven to 325°F. Place all the ingredients in a large, heavy, ovenproof pot. Bring to a boil over high heat. Cover and place in the oven. Cook for 1 hour.

Serve with brown rice.

Spinach, Potato and Lentil Stew

SERVES 6

VEGETARIANS WILL REVEL IN THIS satisfying stew that is power-packed with protein from lentils and tofu. Whether the red, yellow, orange or green form of this ancient legume is used, lentils can be soaked or not, according to how much time you have. Soaking will hasten the actual cooking time by about 15 minutes. Tofu, however, is pre-cooked and needs only be tossed into the skillet with the seasonings until heated through thoroughly. Enjoy the surprise of fresh oranges flavoring this stew.

2 tablespoons olive oil

1 large onion, thinly sliced

2 cloves garlic, minced

1 teaspoon ground cumin

1 teaspoon ground coriander

2 large potatoes, cut into 1-inch dice

2 pounds spinach, washed well

1 quart water

1 cup lentils, rinsed

1 pound extra-firm tofu, cut into 1-inch dice

2 navel oranges, sectioned

Salt to taste

In a deep, heavy skillet place the olive oil, onion, garlic, cumin, coriander and potatoes and sauté over medium heat until the potatoes are browned, about 10 minutes. Add the spinach, water, lentils and tofu. Gently simmer for 30 minutes. Add more water if the stew becomes too dry. In the last 5 minutes carefully stir in the orange sections. Adjust seasoning to taste with salt.

Serve with warmed pita bread.

Autumn Vegetable Stew

SERVES 6

PUMPKINS HAVE MORE USES in October than merely serving as jack-o-lanterns. They're delicious and can be used like a large squash. Combined with Autumn's harvest of vegetables such as butternut squash, turnips, parsnips and leeks, they make a splendid seasonal stew. Add the sweetness of apples and tomatoes with a splash of maple syrup and the traditional "pumpkin pie" spices, and this thick, savory stew will be a winner all winter long.

10 ounces butternut squash, peeled, seeded, cut into 1-inch cubes

10 ounces pumpkin, peeled, seeded, cut into 1-inch cubes

 2 turnips, peeled, cut into 1-inch cubes

 1 large parsnip, peeled, cut into 1-inch pieces

 4 tablespoons unsalted butter

 1 large leek, thinly sliced, washed well

 2 tablespoons flour

 1 teaspoon ground cinnamon

¼ teaspoon ground cloves

¼ teaspoon ground allspice

 1 28-ounce can tomatoes

 1 teaspoon salt

 1 tablespoon maple syrup

 1 cup apple cider

 2 tart apples, peeled, cored, quartered, thinly sliced

Place the butternut squash, pumpkin, turnips and parsnip in a large pot and cover with water. Bring to a boil, then lower the heat and simmer for about 15 minutes, until the vegetables are almost tender. Drain into a large bowl and reserve the cooking liquid.

In a medium skillet over low heat, melt 2 tablespoons of the butter and add the leek. Cover and cook for 10 minutes.

Place the vegetables and the leek back into the large pot. Add the remaining butter to the skillet and add the flour, cinnamon, cloves and allspice. Cook the roux over medium heat until it is light brown, about 6 to 10 minutes. Add to the pot of vegetables. Add the tomatoes, crushing them with your hands as you do, and 3 cups of the vegetable cooking water. Cover and cook over medium heat for about 10 minutes, until the stew is thick and simmering. Add the salt, maple syrup, cider and apples and cook for 10 minutes more.

Serve with a basket of warm cinnamon rolls.

Caribbean Fish and Sausage Stew

SERVES 6

CARIBBEAN CUISINE REFLECTS A rich blend of culinary traditions from native islanders in the West Indies, to African, Spanish, Dutch, American and British colonial residents. With its emphasis on fresh seafood, spicy soups, tropical fruits, coconut and one-pot dishes, I've found Caribbean cuisine one of the most exciting to cook-and-eat. This stew, combining spicy chorizo sausage with chunks of hearty white fish and rice, is a perfect example.

2 onions, chopped

2 cloves garlic, minced

1 jalapeño pepper, seeded, finely chopped

2 tablespoons corn oil

2½ cups rice

2 quarts chicken broth

2 pounds firm white fish fillets, cut into 1-inch cubes

1 pound chorizo sausage, sliced ½-inch thick

1 bay leaf

Chopped fresh cilantro for garnish

In a large, heavy pot, sauté the onions, garlic, and jalapeño pepper in the corn oil for 2 minutes. Stir in the rice and cook for 5 minutes. Add 1¼ cups of the stock and cook over high heat until the liquid is absorbed. Lower the heat to low and add the remaining broth, fish, sausage and bay leaf. Cover and cook for 15 minutes, until the fish is flaky and the rice is tender. Sprinkle with cilantro before serving.

Serve with a basket of fried plantains. To prepare, cut unripe plantains very thin, on the bias, and soak in salted water for an hour. Heat 2 inches of corn oil over high heat. Drain and pat dry the plantain slices and fry, a few at a time, in the hot oil until golden. Drain, sprinkle with coarse salt and serve.

Desert Island Tuna

SERVES 4 TO 6

OF COURSE, CLEVER COOKS WILL FIND a way to turn any ingredient into a stew. While tuna is unexpected in this stew, simmering the dense, meaty fish with an assortment of chopped carrots, celery, mushrooms and fresh tomatoes is a standard stewpot technique. Add anchovy paste, a splash of white wine and dried basil to accent the delicate flavors of this versatile fish from the Pacific Ocean.

½ cup chopped onions

3 tablespoons olive oil

2 pounds tuna steaks, cut into 2-inch cubes

½ cup diced carrots

½ cup diced celery

1 cup sliced mushrooms

½ cup chopped tomato

2 tablespoons anchovy paste

1 tablespoon dried basil

1 cup dry white wine

1 cup fish broth

In a deep, wide skillet over medium heat, sauté the onions in the olive oil for 5 minutes. Add the tuna pieces and cook on all sides for 7 to 10 minutes. Stir in the carrots, celery, and mushrooms, and cook for 5 more minutes. Add the remaining ingredients, bring to a simmer, cover and cook for 20 to 30 minutes, or until the fish is flaky.

Serve with whole wheat quick bread (see recipe on page 123).

Clam and Corn Stew

SERVES 4 TO 6

ALMOST A CHOWDER, except for the missing potatoes, this meatless stew packed with clams is utterly delicious. If possible, to enjoy the fullest flavor, cut the kernels off freshly cooked corn on the cob; one ear makes approximately one half cup of kernels. Chicken broth can be used successfully instead of fish broth. Do not overcook the stew or the clams will become tough. Like most soups and stews with seafood, this one is best if eaten the same day it's prepared.

3 ears corn

1 onion

4 cloves garlic, minced

2 tablespoons corn oil

1 quart fish broth or bottled clam juice

¼ cup butter

¼ cup flour

2 cups shucked littleneck clams

¼ cup chopped fresh parsley

Salt to taste

Cut the kernels off the cobs and set aside. In a deep, heavy pot over medium heat, sauté the onion and garlic in the corn oil for 5 minutes. Add the fish broth and the corn cobs. Raise the heat to high and boil the broth until it reduces by half.

In a small, heavy skillet, melt the butter over low heat and then whisk in the flour. Cook the roux for 5 minutes. Strain the broth over a large bowl and discard the solids. Remove the roux from the heat and gradually whisk in a cup or two of the broth. Slowly add the roux back into the broth, return the liquid to the pot and bring to a boil over medium heat for 10 minutes. Add the clams and corn and simmer for 5 minutes. Sprinkle with the parsley and adjust the flavor with salt.

Serve with oat muffins (see recipe on page 125).

Italian Salmon Stew

SERVES 6

ITALIANS LOVE SALMON AS PASSIONATELY as Pacific-Northwesterners or Scandinavians do. Its rich taste balances the intense flavors of such basic Italian ingredients as garlic, olive oil and onion. In this recipe the succulent fish adapts readily to the flavors of a tomato and wine sauce accented with chopped walnuts. Like most fish, salmon is ideal for simmering in a stew because it remains tender and moist at low cooking temperatures. Just watch carefully so you don't overcook the fish, and serve immediately once it's removed from the heat.

2	cloves garlic
¼	cup olive oil
1	onion, chopped
2	tablespoons chopped fresh parsley
2	cups peeled and chopped tomatoes
¼	cup finely chopped walnuts
1¼	cups dry white wine
3	pounds salmon fillets, cut into 2-inch pieces
1	bay leaf
½	teaspoon salt

In a large, heavy pot, over medium heat, sauté the garlic in the olive oil until browned. Discard the garlic. Add the onion and cook for 5 minutes. Add the parsley, tomatoes, walnuts and wine. Simmer for 15 minutes. Add the fish, bay leaf and salt and continue to simmer for 15 minutes, until the fish is just tender.

Serve with warm focaccia (see recipe on page 124).

Fisher's Island Stew

SERVES 4 TO 6

FISHER'S ISLAND IS A LARGE ISLAND in Long Island Sound just off the Connecticut coast, one of those idyllic summer places where the same families have vacationed for generations. The island's general store stocks every dry good imaginable—from pistachios and pie plates to light bulbs and ice cream—plus an abundance of fresh seafood that has inspired many fish stews. A stew of fresh cod or striped bass steeped in a fragrant tomato broth with garlic, leeks and herbs for seasoning is a fond memory for many summer folk.

3	cloves garlic, minced
1	leek, chopped, well rinsed
1/3	cup olive oil
1/2	teaspoon dried marjoram
1/4	teaspoon dried tarragon
1 1/2	cups dry white wine
20	ounces canned chopped tomatoes with their juices
1	teaspoon freshly ground pepper
1/2	teaspoon salt
1	pound cod fillets, cut into 2-inch pieces
1	pound striped bass fillets, cut into 2-inch pieces
12	littleneck clams, well scrubbed
1/4	cup chopped fresh parsley

Preheat the oven to 350°F.

In a large, heavy pot, fitted with a lid, sauté the garlic and leek in the olive oil, over medium heat for 5 minutes. Stir in the marjoram and tarragon and cook for 3 minutes. Add the wine, tomatoes, pepper, salt, cod and striped bass, and raise the heat to high so that the stew boils. Cover and place in the oven for 20 minutes. Remove from the oven and mix in the clams. Replace the lid and cook in the oven for another 10 minutes, or until the clams are open. Sprinkle with the chopped parsley.

Serve with white rice.

'Sconset Stew

SERVES 6 TO 8

SUMMERS BY THE SHORE JUST NATURALLY *inspire meals from the sea and this coastal stew, named for Siasconset on Natucket Island, celebrates the delectable shellfish found along the Eastern Seaboard. It's a seafood stew akin to San Francisco's acclaimed cioppino or France's bouillabaise and it's packed with clams, scallops and crabmeat in a tomato broth. The good news: this stew will feed a crowd, so make a pot ahead or, on the same day, and have a rollicking summer beach house party.*

3	tablespoons butter
1	onion, diced
2	cloves garlic, minced
¼	teaspoon crumbled saffron
2	stalks celery, sliced
1	teaspoon thyme
2	cups fish broth or bottled clam juice
1	14-ounce can crushed tomatoes with their juices
2	pounds bay scallops
12	cherrystone clams
1	pound lump crabmeat
⅓	cup chopped fresh chives

In a large, heavy pot fitted with a lid, melt the butter over medium heat. Add the onion, garlic and saffron and sauté for 5 minutes. Stir in the celery and thyme and cook for another 3 minutes. Mix in the fish broth and tomatoes, and raise the heat until the stew boils. Stir in the scallops and clams and cover with the lid. When the stew begins to boil again, lower the heat to a simmer and cook for 10 minutes, or until the clams are open. Gently mix in the crabmeat and simmer until heated through, about 3 minutes. Sprinkle with the chives.

Serve with warm oat muffins (see recipe on page 125).

Shrimp Etouffée

SERVES 6

CAJUN COOKING, SPIKED BY the heat of Tabasco sauce and linked to the French homeland of Arcadian immigrants from Canada, is one of America's most celebrated regional cuisines. Along Louisiana's Gulf Coast, French Arcadian influences mingle with Spanish and Creole cookery traditions, many of these from Africa, to create a rich culinary legacy. Be prepared for some fire in this seafood dish served over rice, a favorite pairing of Cajun cooks.

2	pounds large shrimp, peeled, deveined
3	tablespoons Creole seasoning
½	cup corn oil
1	cup flour
2	small green peppers, diced
1	large onion, diced
1	large celery stalk, sliced
3	cloves garlic, minced
12	ounces dark beer
2	bay leaves
3	cups chicken broth
2	teaspoons hot pepper sauce (such as Tabasco)
2	tablespoons Worcestershire sauce
1	teaspoon salt
3	scallions, sliced

Place the shrimp in a medium-sized bowl and sprinkle with 1 tablespoon of the Creole seasoning. Set aside.

Heat the corn oil and flour in a large, heavy pot, over medium heat. Stir until it forms a paste and add the green peppers, onion, celery, garlic and the 2 remaining tablespoons of Creole seasoning. Cook until the onions are clear, about 7 to 10 minutes. Remove from the heat and beat in the beer, whisking until smooth. Return to the heat and add the bay leaves. Whisk in the broth, hot pepper sauce, Worcestershire sauce and salt. Add the shrimp and simmer until the shrimp turns a coral pink, about 10 minutes. Before serving, sprinkle with the scallions.

Serve over rice.

Grouper Creole

SERVES 6

THERE ARE SEVERAL GROUPER SPECIES native to the Caribbean. They all have firm, flaky flesh and an appealing taste. Sometimes known as giant sea bass, they are versatile enough to match the intense flavors of sautéed garlic, onions, tomato paste and bell peppers seasoned with traditional bayou country spices like cumin, oregano and wine. Serve this dish Louisiana-style over rice for a wonderful one-dish meal.

2 pounds skinless boneless grouper fillets, cut into 2-inch squares

6 cloves garlic, minced

3 tablespoons fresh lime juice

½ teaspoon salt

¼ teaspoon freshly ground pepper

⅓ cup flour

3 tablespoons olive oil

1 small onion, thinly sliced

1 small green bell pepper, seeded, thinly sliced

½ teaspoon ground cumin

1 teaspoon dried oregano

¼ cup tomato paste

1 teaspoon red wine vinegar

½ cup dry white wine

1 bay leaf

2 tablespoons finely chopped fresh Italian parsley

Rinse the fillets and pat dry. In a medium bowl, toss with half the garlic, lime juice, salt and pepper. Marinate for 15 minutes.

Remove the fish from the marinade and dredge in the flour. Shake off the excess. In a large skillet, over medium heat, brown the fish in the oil on both sides, about 3 to 5 minutes. Remove the fish from the skillet and drain on paper towels.

In the same skillet, over medium heat, sauté the remaining garlic, onion, bell pepper, cumin, and oregano for 5 minutes. Add the tomato paste and cook for 1 minute more. Stir in the vinegar, wine and bay leaf and mix well.

Place the fish in the sauce and simmer gently for 7 to 10 minutes, until the fish is opaque. If necessary, add a little more wine to the sauce. Remove the bay leaf and sprinkle with the Italian parsley.

Serve over rice.

Accompaniments

Garlic Bread	Buttermilk Biscuits
Corn Bread	Focaccia
Whole Wheat Quick Bread	Oat Muffins
Cheese Toasts	Hush Puppies

Garlic Bread

SERVES 6

1 18-inch loaf Italian or French bread

2 tablespoons garlic powder

2 tablespoons dried parsley

½ cup butter

⅓ cup olive oil

½ cup grated parmesan cheese

Cut the loaf of bread in half, lengthwise. Place the butter, garlic powder, olive oil, and parsley in a small sauce pot, over medium heat, until butter is melted. Spoon the mixture over the cut side of the bread. Sprinkle with the cheese.

Place the bread, cut side up, on a baking sheet and put under a broiler for 3 to 5 minutes, until the bread is bubbling and lightly browned. Remove from the oven and cut into 1-inch slices and serve.

Corn Bread

SERVES 6

¾ cup flour

1 teaspoon salt

1 cup milk

2 tablespoons maple syrup

1½ cup cornmeal

2 eggs, beaten

2 tablespoons corn oil

Preheat the oven to 400°F. Place the dry ingredients in a medium bowl and combine well with a wire whisk. Add the eggs, milk and oil and mix until smooth. Butter a 10-inch, cast-iron pan, or a 8 x 10-inch baking pan and pour in the batter. Drizzle the maple syrup over the batter and bake in the oven for 30 minutes, until the top is lightly browned. Cut into 2-inch squares and serve warm.

Whole Wheat Quick Bread

MAKES 1 LOAF (SERVES 6)

½ cup whole wheat flour

⅔ cup all-purpose flour

2 teaspoons baking powder

½ teaspoon salt

½ teaspoon pepper

1 egg

⅔ cup milk

3 tablespoons corn oil

2 tablespoons molasses

Preheat oven to 375°F. Coat a 5 x 9 x 3-inch loaf pan with butter. Using a wire whisk, combine the dry ingredients in a large bowl. In a small bowl, whisk together the remaining ingredients. Pour the wet ingredients into the dry and mix until just combined. The batter will be quite lumpy. Pour the batter into the prepared pan and bake for 25 minutes, until lightly browned.

Cheese Toasts

SERVES 6

6 slices multi grain or sour dough bread

1 cup shredded mixed cheeses (such as cheddar, mozzarella, blue)

Sprinkle of paprika or parsley for garnish

Lightly toast the bread and then place on a baking sheet lined with aluminum foil. Cover each slice with the shredded cheese. Sprinkle with the paprika or parsley. Place 4-inches under a broiler until the cheese has melted completely. Remove from the broiler, cut each slice in half on the diagonal and serve immediately.

Buttermilk Biscuits

MAKES 12 TO 16 BISCUITS

2 cups flour

2 teaspoons baking powder

½ teaspoon salt

2 teaspoons sugar

½ cup unsalted butter

⅔ cup buttermilk

Preheat the oven to 425°F. Place the dry ingredients in a medium bowl and mix well with a wire whisk. Using a pastry cutter or two knives, cut in the butter until the mixture resembles coarse meal. Stir in the buttermilk, and then turn onto a floured surface and knead a few times. Either roll out the dough to ½-inch thickness and use a 2-inch cutter to form rounds, or pull off pieces of the dough and roll them into balls and flatten by hand. Place the biscuits on a buttered baking sheet and bake for 15 minutes. Serve warm.

Focaccia

SERVES 6

1 15-ounce pre-made pizza dough

Flour

1 teaspoon dry rosemary, crumbled

1 tablespoon grated Parmesan cheese

2 teaspoons minced garlic

1 tablespoon finely chopped onion

1 tablespoon coarse salt

Preheat the oven to 425°F. Flatten the dough on a lightly floured surface. Sprinkle with the rosemary, cheese, garlic and onion and knead until well incorporated. Place on a baking sheet lined with parchment paper. Press the dough into a circle about 12-inches around and ½-inch thick. Prick well all over with a fork and sprinkle with salt. Bake for 20 minutes. Cut into 12 wedges and serve warm.

Oat Muffins

MAKES 12 MUFFINS

1 cup instant oatmeal

½ cup all-purpose flour

½ cup whole wheat flour

3 tablespoons brown sugar

1 tablespoon baking powder

1 teaspoon salt

1 egg

1 cup apple juice

¼ cup corn oil

Preheat the oven to 425°F. Coat 12 3-inch muffin tins with butter or line with paper baking cups. Using a wire whisk, combine the dry ingredients in a large bowl. In a small bowl, whisk together the remaining ingredients. Pour the wet ingredients into the dry and mix until just combined. The mixture will be quite lumpy. Spoon the batter into the prepared tins ¾ filled. Bake for 20 to 22 minutes, until the muffins are springy to the touch.

Hush Puppies

SERVES 6 (2 HUSHPUPPIES EACH)

1⅔ cups stone ground, white or
      yellow corn meal

⅓ cup all purpose flour

2 teaspoons baking powder

½ teaspoon baking soda

2 teaspoons sugar

1 teaspoon salt

2 eggs, beaten

1 cup buttermilk

½ cup minced onions

Corn oil for frying

Place 2-inches of oil in a heavy, deep skillet. Heat oil to 360°F. In a small bowl, whisk together the dry ingredients. Add the wet ingredients and mix until just combined. Drop rounded tablespoons of batter into the hot oil, being sure not to crowd the pan, and cook for 2 minutes. Remove with a slotted spoon onto paper towels and keep warm in a 200°F oven. Serve piping hot.

Index